Righting Wrongs

20
HUMAN RIGHTS
HEROES AROUND
THE WORLD

ROBIN KIRK

CHIC
REVI
PRES

D1417306

Copyright © 2022 by Robin Kirk
Published by Chicago Review Press Incorporated
814 North Franklin Street
Chicago, Illinois 60610
ISBN 978-1-64160-559-5

Library of Congress Control Number: 2022930176

Cover and interior illustrations: Ana Paiva
Cover and interior design: Sadie Teper

Printed in the United States of America
5 4 3 2 1

To Frances and Ray

An extra miracle, extra and ordinary:
the unthinkable
can be thought.

—"Miracle Fair" by Wisława Szymborska (Poland), translated
from the Polish by Clare Cavanagh and Stanisław Barańczak

Wisława Szymborska (1923–2012) was born in Poland and
worked as a poetry editor, translator, and columnist. She was
awarded the Nobel Prize in Literature in 1996.

PAULI MURRAY
Durham, NC, US

JUDITH HEUMANN
New York City, NY, US

EGLANTYNE JEBB
Ellesmere, United Kingdom

S. JAMES ANAYA
Santa Clara, NM, US

RALPH J. BUNCHE
Los Angeles, CA, US

JODY WILLIAMS
Brattleboro, VT, US

**CATHERINE
COLEMAN FLOWERS**
Blackbelt, AL, US

BERTA CÁCERES
La Esperanza, Honduras

FANNYANN EDDY
Freetown, Sierra Leone

VÍCTOR JARA
Santiago, Chile

JUAN E. MÉNDEZ
Mar del Plata, Argentina

INGRID NEWKIRK
Kingston upon Thames,
United Kingdom

FRIDTJOF NANSEN
Oslo, Norway

BENJAMIN B. FERENCZ
Csolt, Hungary

**ANNA
POLITKOVSKAYA**
Moscow, Russia

P. C. CHANG
Tientsin, China

CARLOS PEÑA RÓMULO
Manila, Philippines

SHIRIN EBADI
Tehran, Iran

HANSA MEHTA
Mumbai, India

HENRI DUNANT
Geneva, Switzerland

CONTENTS

INTRODUCTION

When I lived in Peru, I often wondered what the land had looked like before Europeans carried out a brutal conquest. Peru's desert coast lifts abruptly into the Andes mountains in dizzyingly steep peaks and canyons. Further east, the mountains plunge into the green immensity of the Amazon jungle.

Preconquest, as many as 14 million people lived under Inca rule in Peru. The Inca empire was prosperous, with stone roads and bridges linking cities and towns. A vast network of irrigation canals watered crops no European would recognize: potatoes, tomatoes, hot peppers, quinoa, and corn. Herds of camel-like llama and vicuña roamed the high plains and were used for their wool and meat and as beasts of burden. In the cities, massive temples of closely fitted stone rose over prosperous streets. Inside, images of gods made of gold gleamed in torchlight.

All of that began to change when Christopher Columbus made landfall in the Americas in 1492. He'd been looking for a route to the spices and silks of the Far East. Instead, his arrival marked devastation for Indigenous peoples and spectacular profits for many Europeans, who immediately began to exploit the so-called New World for its riches.

Along with horses, guns, and religion, the Europeans brought new diseases that spread far beyond their ships. In what is now modern-day Peru, a mysterious "delirious fever"—possibly smallpox—killed the

Inca king sometime between 1525 and 1527. Two of his sons fought to replace him. One, Atahualpa, had just defeated his brother in battle when Spanish adventurer Francisco Pizarro landed near the modern town of Tumbes in 1532.

News of the Spaniards' arrival reached Atahualpa as he rested at the town of Cajamarca. Curious, he invited them to his court. He wasn't afraid. After all, thousands of loyal, armed, battle-hardened soldiers protected him. His spies reported that the strangers had just 110 infantrymen, 67 cavalrymen (and their horses, a curiosity), 3 guns, and 2 small cannons.

But as Atahualpa arrived to greet them in Cajamarca's central square, the Spaniards launched a desperate ambush. In a matter of hours, Pizarro and his men slaughtered hundreds of Atahualpa's soldiers. And they seized the Inca king himself, demanding gold as ransom for sparing his life.

For weeks, the terrified people piled up all the gold they could collect. But Pizarro had lied about his intentions. On August 29, 1533, he ordered Atahualpa executed. He wanted the Inca empire for himself and for Spain.

The Inca were no strangers to conquest. Like European monarchs, they believed conquest was a divine right. Over the previous centuries, the Inca had conquered dozens of smaller groups, demanding payments and obedience in return for sparing their lives. Some Indigenous Peruvians helped Pizarro as a way of freeing themselves from Inca oppression.

But there the similarities between Inca conquest and Spanish conquest end. Europeans had a very different view of what conquest meant. Indigenous communities that had farmed shared plots for generations soon learned that the Spanish king—who never even visited the Americas—suddenly owned their land. Farmers owed him and his nobles not only their labor but also most of what they mined, harvested, or grew.

Unscrupulous foreigners killed and raped without any fear of punishment. No longer could Indigenous people worship their own gods. The Catholic priests who accompanied the conquistadores forcibly converted thousands, often at sword point, and outlawed any vestige of traditional faith upon pain of death.

Most Europeans would not have found anything strange about the conquest of the Americas. Tales of seizing the lands of others, enslaving them, exterminating their beliefs, and looting their belongings had filled Europe's history books for centuries.

But just because something is normal or expected doesn't make it right. Shockingly—amazingly, miraculously—some people raised their voices to protest what was happening to Indigenous America. Two men—one a Spanish priest and the other an Indigenous writer and artist—spoke powerfully about the injustices of the conquest and the rights of Indigenous people. Then both of them did something to translate their beliefs into action.

To be sure, this wasn't the first time someone had questioned violence against others or tried to advance the idea of rights. I highlight this moment for what it teaches about the human rights heroes I profile in these pages. In essence, human rights are rooted in the constant human debate over what is right and what is wrong. The heroes in these pages perceived a wrong that few others recognized. Then they worked to convince others to respect an oppressed group's human rights.

Human rights are never fixed, in other words. There is always a new way of thinking about rights that advances protections to people—or animals or the earth itself—and improves life for all.

Father Bartolomé de Las Casas was perhaps the most prominent person to question the conquest and stand up for the rights of Indigenous people. A Spanish priest, he disembarked at the New World port of Santo Domingo (now the capital of the Dominican Republic) in 1502 and took part in the conquest of modern-day Cuba. He also owned an *encomienda*, a plantation with Indigenous indentured laborers.

These were families that had, before the conquest, worked the land as a community and without individual property rights. After the conquest, they were compelled to work the land for European landowners.

For a time, Las Casas accepted the brutality he witnessed against Indigenous Americans as natural, even necessary. Spanish law gave so-called civilized peoples, or Christians, the right to wage war upon so-called uncivilized peoples without any fear of punishment.

But gradually, Las Casas started to question the savagery of what he saw and heard. Heavily armed Spaniards would massacre whole villages, enslave the survivors, and mutilate anyone who rebelled by cutting off their hands. Was it necessary, he wondered, to slaughter defenseless women and children? Sometimes, he later wrote, Spaniards murdered people as if it were a sport. Spaniards began "to exercise their bloody Butcheries and Strategems, and overrunning their Cities and Towns, spar'd no Age, or Sex, nay not so much as Women with Child."

Unlike most of the Europeans around him, Las Casas came to see Indigenous people not as enslaved people or animals but as human beings. Instead of dangerous "others," these were men, women, and children like himself and his Spanish family.

It's important to recognize that Las Casas continued to embrace European superiority and believed that Christians should convert "heathens" to save their souls. For a time, he supported importing enslaved people from Africa to the Americas, an opinion he came to deeply regret.

Yet he also saw what so many others didn't: that Indigenous people were also human beings deserving of rights. This was both a deeply personal realization and the beginning of a profound change in how Las Casas lived. At age 30, he gave up his *encomienda* and the Indigenous workers there and later refused to grant forgiveness to any Christian who did not do the same.

His passion often irritated his colleagues. Once, a bishop grew tired of Las Casas's protest of the deaths of thousands of Indigenous children. "What is that to me and to the king?" the bishop asked him.

Las Casas responded, "What is it to your lordship and to the king that those souls die? Oh, great and eternal God! Who is there to whom that *is* something?"

Las Casas spent the rest of his life writing dozens of books and letters exposing the atrocities of the conquest. He also traveled between the Americas and Spain to try and convince the king and his advisers to curb abuses against Indigenous peoples. Among his most famous books is *In Defense of the Indians*, which remains widely studied today.

In his life, I see questions that continue to shape the lives of the human rights heroes in this book. Who counts as fully human? Who and what, including animals, plants, and even our environment, should have rights? Once an injustice is identified, what will people do to address it and make the world a better place?

Las Casas's views reflected who he was: a White, Spanish, educated, wealthy man of the cloth. A very different voice emerged soon after Atahualpa's murder. Felipe Guáman Poma de Ayala was a minor noble born in 1535 to an Indigenous community the Inca had conquered. In Quechua, the Inca language, his name translates as Falcon Cougar.

As a matter of survival, Falcon Cougar learned to write and speak Spanish. He converted to Christianity (whether this was a free choice is unknown) and worked as a secretary to a Spanish priest. As an Indigenous person, he personally suffered the injustices of the conquest and the oppression of his own people.

Perhaps for that reason, Falcon Cougar's views were much more radical than those of Las Casas. He never questioned his own humanity or the idea that Indigenous people should have rights. The conquest was not merely brutal, he argued. Subjugating another people, stealing their lands and wealth, and robbing them of control over their communities were wrong. He became so passionate about Spain's abuses that he did something remarkable: Falcon Cougar wrote a letter.

In today's world, that may not seem a radical act. But at the time, letters were a powerful way to communicate. In Falcon Cougar's case, the letter was also quite a feat. The Inca empire had no written language. If a message needed to be sent, a quipu was prepared, a kind of necklace made of elaborately knotted string, with each element having a specific meaning. Falcon Cougar had learned not only to put pen to paper and speak Spanish but also to draw what he was seeing.

Falcon Cougar went far beyond anything Las Casas had written. His letter, which he titled "New Chronicle and Good Government," is one of the most spectacular letters ever written. In over 1,000 handwritten pages, Falcon Cougar argued to the Spanish king that the conquest itself was wrong. The Spanish government was wrong. The merchants profiting from the plunder were wrong. Even the pope, the ultimate religious authority for Christians, was wrong.

Indigenous people, Falcon Cougar argued, had rights equal to those of the Europeans. Indeed, they were equal in every way to Whites.

Along with a history of Peru and a survey of Inca culture, Falcon Cougar included 398 of his own line drawings. Some represented former Inca leaders. Others showed farming methods or religious ceremonies. Still others depicted abuses committed by the Spanish, including the execution of Atahualpa and the burning of families in their homes. For people at the time, these were the equivalent of photographs or even news reports of atrocities.

Like any skilled human rights advocate, Falcon Cougar even offered the king a solution to the evils of the conquest. The Spanish should immediately cease violent acts and seek a diplomatic agreement that would recognize Indigenous independence. All should have equal rights.

With his writing and constant lobbying of the king and his advisors, Las Casas succeeded in convincing the Spanish monarchy to implement some reforms. Tragically, Falcon Cougar's letter never reached Spain. An ambassador likely transported "New Chronicle and Good Government" to Europe but may have been too afraid to deliver it to the king. In 1908 a researcher discovered the water-damaged pages in the Danish Royal Archive.

Yet there's a powerful and positive lesson to be taken from the stories of Falcon Cougar, Las Casas, and the heroes in this book. Often, the work of defending human rights is hard and seems ineffective, at least at first. Many of the people profiled in these pages never saw the results of their advocacy—or were killed for calling out injustice. Some, such as Bartolomé de Las Casas, did see improvements, though not as much as they desired.

Yet all of them understood that action matters. Doing something matters. Seeing a wrong and attempting to correct it matters. As one hero, Catherine Coleman Flowers, told me, "We may not change everything, but we're going to change something." The only way the world changes for the better is when people act.

Today, that same belief that wrongs must be righted provides a common language for social justice movements around the globe. After two devastating world wars, the international community came together to create the United Nations (UN) and then, in 1948, both the Universal Declaration of Human Rights and the Convention on the Prevention and Punishment of the Crime of Genocide. With 30 articles, the declaration sets a foundation—but not a ceiling—for human rights.

Since then, people have come together to establish new interpretations of the declaration, including rights for LGBTQ, Indigenous, and disability communities. In this book's chapters, you'll also hear voices promoting new ideas of rights, including those for animals and the planet.

Building on the legacies of Bartolomé de Las Casas and Falcon Cougar, the heroes in the following pages saw an injustice, figured out how to correct it, and acted. They would be the first to say that they weren't alone in their quests. Human rights thrive only if people—including you and me—make them thrive.

The human rights challenges that face us are as serious today as when Pizarro first set foot on Peru's Pacific coast. Children continue to be recruited as child soldiers; refugees continue to be denied asylum; and people are still tortured, executed, wrongly imprisoned, and discriminated against for who they are, the color of their skin, where they were born, or what they believe.

Yet there are heroes among us who challenge us to see change as not only possible but also imperative. In this book's chapters, you'll read about a hero who began a movement to end terrible living and labor conditions for children. Another insisted on the rights of former colonies to independence. Another dedicated his life to Indigenous people, who are gradually reclaiming the right to control their ancestral lands.

For the most part, these people have yet to be fully recognized for their crucial contributions to human rights. Many are American, either via birth or naturalization. Others hail from the Philippines, Sierra Leone, Norway, and Argentina. Eleven are women, including one person whom we now might call transgender. Twelve are people of color. One is lesbian. Another campaigns for rights from a wheelchair. Two identify as Indigenous. One is Muslim, one is Hindu, and one is Buddhist. Others claim no religion at all. There are journalists, soldiers, lawyers, priests, teachers, former law enforcement officers, and explorers. Two survived torture. Several were refugees.

Some were killed for their human rights work. Those chapters were especially hard to write.

Some of the stories are uplifting. Some are heavy with the hard work that was cut off too soon or remains unfinished. But running through these stories is a tough thread, a passion, and a light that unites us across time, place, and generation: the conviction that we as individuals can and should and must do the work to make the world a better place.

Robin Kirk
Durham, NC

THE MAN IN WHITE: HENRI DUNANT

🚩 **THE LAWS OF WAR**

👤 **1828-1910**

📍 **SWITZERLAND**

> *By Thy power, let*
> *there be peace, O God!*

Humans have always waged war. And they've always had rules of war that all sides understand even when they don't necessarily obey.

Until the 20th century, rules of war did little to prevent human suffering. To the contrary, some rules created massive suffering. Armies knew the rules allowed them to burn whole towns to the ground. Civilians—people who take no part in fighting—could be killed or enslaved. Many soldiers were mercenaries, fighting for personal gain. Others were untrained and poorly equipped. Echoing Thucydides, himself a soldier of ancient Greece and a historian, people generally agreed that "the strong do what they can and the weak suffer what they must."

But in June 1859, one person began what would become a massive change. A Swiss banker and businessman started to argue for new rules of war that would save lives. Henri Dunant succeeded in planting the

1

seed for an organization that would fundamentally change the way most wars are fought, protecting the lives of soldiers and civilians alike.

Dunant was an unlikely activist. At 31, he had generous sideburns, called mutton chops (after cuts of sheep meat), and the ample belly of a prosperous businessman. He'd been a pampered and delicate child who seemed never to have wanted more than to join the family business as a merchant. His one passion was his Protestant faith and volunteering for charities in his home city of Geneva, Switzerland.

Dunant was making his way through Italy with business in mind. The French emperor, Napoleon III, was camped with his army near the village of Solferino. Dunant wanted a meeting with him, planning to convince the emperor to invest in grain from Algeria to ship to Europe. Basically, Dunant wanted to make money from the war Napoleon III was fighting against a rival, Franz Joseph I, emperor of the Austro-Hungarian empire.

THE ENLIGHTENMENT

Many important human rights ideas emerged during the Enlightenment, a period covering the 17th and 18th centuries. These ideas can be seen in documents like the English Bill of Rights, the American Constitution and Bill of Rights, and the French Declaration of the Rights of Man.

The Italians were fighting to free themselves from the Austrians. Napoleon III thought that by helping them, he'd weaken his rival emperor. European battles could be quite formal, with officers dressed in brightly colored uniforms leading thousands of men in neat lines. As Dunant neared Solferino on June 24, 1859, fighting broke out between approximately 170,000 uniformed Austrian soldiers and a similar number of allied French and Italians.

The fighting quickly turned gruesome. By the end of the day, more than 6,000 soldiers lay dead. Another 30,000 were wounded and abandoned on the battlefield, equivalent to the undergraduate enrollment at many American universities. Some soldiers executed wounded enemies or left their own comrades to die. Neither army had enough medical staff to even bring the wounded something to drink in the brutally hot summer sun.

NAPOLEON AND NAPOLEON III

The differences between Napoleons can be confusing. Napoleon III was the nephew of Napoleon Bonaparte, a French military leader and later emperor from 1804 until 1814 and again in 1815. Napoleon Bonaparte died in exile in 1821. Napoleon III was France's last emperor, defeated by the Prussians in 1870.

Dunant arrived too late for the battle, but he witnessed the aftermath. In his white suit, he walked through blood-stained fields. Solferino was no different from any other battle that decade or even century, with horrific casualties and little effort to help the wounded. But the sights, sounds, and smells were new to Dunant. "Bodies of men and horses covered the battlefield," he later wrote. "Corpses were strewn over roads, ditches, ravines, thickets and fields; the approaches to Solferino were literally thick with dead."

CRUSADING NURSES

In the Crimea in the 1850s, allied British and French forces battled the Russian Empire, causing heavy casualties among soldiers and civilians. Florence Nightingale worked as a nurse at a British hospital in what is now Istanbul, Turkey. Upon arrival, she was stunned to discover that the hospital sat above filthy water and was infested with rats and other vermin.

Nightingale developed many sanitation practices—scrubbing floors and beds, washing hands, and providing clean water—reducing death rates by two-thirds. Her innovations spurred similar changes in medical facilities around the world and remain in use today.

Much as Nightingale had in the Crimea, Clara Barton helped change medical practices in the United States during the Civil War. She collected supplies and worked as a nurse in army field hospitals and on battlefields to tend the wounded. Once the war ended, she set up a system for families to find missing loved ones. Barton later helped found the American Red Cross and advocated for the passage of new laws of war to protect civilians.

While the International Committee of the Red Cross helps civilians and prisoners of war internationally, national Red Cross societies assist during natural disasters like hurricanes or earthquakes. Often, Red Cross societies collect needed supplies, including blood donations, to be stored and used when needed.

Dunant had no medical skills. He was neither French, Italian, nor Austrian. But he decided that it didn't matter who the soldiers were or what side they'd fought on. They needed help. "Certainly I was a tourist," he later wrote, "but a tourist much concerned with questions about humanity."

On his own, Dunant organized food and water for the wounded. Locals, especially women and children, pitched in. With his own money, he bought supplies for doctors. He wrote letters for the dying to their families. A wealthy friend sent money to buy more supplies.

Solferino was not unique. The same military strategies led to immense human suffering during the American Civil War from 1860 to 1865. Just as at Solferino, neither the Confederate nor Union Armies had enough medical workers or supplies to help all the wounded. At the battle of Gettysburg, Pennsylvania, for example, the combined armies abandoned 22,000 wounded soldiers to die on the battlefield.

For Dunant, the lesson was clear. The rules of war had to change. He believed volunteers like himself had the power to make war less horrible. In 1862 Dunant self-published *A Memory of Solferino*, his account of what he'd seen.

He didn't just recount gruesome details. Dunant argued that it was necessary for countries to agree to make conflict less brutal. For instance, he proposed that volunteers could help the wounded regardless of whom they'd fought for. At Solferino, he'd seen thousands of people, mainly women, rescue soldiers, treat their injuries and feed them, and write letters to their loved ones. He wanted to capture this commitment in an international agreement that would formalize new rules of war and create a permanent group to help the wounded, including civilians. "Would it not be possible, in times of peace and quiet, to form relief societies for the purpose of having care given to the wounded in wartime by zealous, devoted, and thoroughly qualified volunteers?" he asked in his memoir.

This was already happening in small ways, he argued. Florence Nightingale, an English nurse, had transformed the way the wounded were treated during the Crimean War in the 1850s. She insisted that hospitals be cleaned and caregivers disinfect soldiers' wounds, practices that continue to save hundreds of thousands of lives a year.

In 1863 Dunant and four other men brought 16 countries together to form what would become the International Committee of the Red Cross (ICRC), headquartered in his native Geneva, Switzerland. The ICRC was among the first nongovernmental organizations (NGOs), or civilians who raise their own money to work on shared problems. (Today, hundreds of NGOs do human rights and humanitarian work.) As one historian put it, "A new movement had been born, in private, among private people and in a small, apparently powerless country, which would soon catch fire among the European rulers before spreading, country by country, throughout the world."

Dunant's timing as a humanitarian was excellent. People were thinking differently about many things. Before Solferino, the campaign to end the slave trade had won over the United Kingdom and France, which outlawed the buying and selling of human beings in 1833 and 1848, respectively. After so many European wars, even kings and queens were questioning more killing, if only to protect their own families and fortunes.

In 1864 Dunant and others combined the ICRC's principles into the first Geneva Convention, or agreement. They wanted governments to enforce care for wounded soldiers, medical facilities, and humanitarian workers. The convention also established the symbol of the ICRC—a red cross.

Over the following decades, new agreements followed, including protections for civilians who take no part in fighting; prisoners of war; and hospitals, museums, and places of worship. Today, the Geneva Conventions also prohibit armies from forcibly moving people as a part of military strategy or to serve as human shields and prohibit rape and the recruitment of children as soldiers. The conventions also prohibit certain weapons, like chemical gases.

Now, internationally agreed-upon symbols—the red cross, the red crescent, the red shield of David, and the red crystal—are accepted as universal emblems of protection in all armed conflicts. Many armies have staff who study the laws of war and advise on actions to make sure soldiers honor the principles Dunant helped establish. Armies that fail to do so not only face condemnation. International and regional courts can now prosecute war crimes and can convict individual officers and force countries to pay victims for what they suffered.

Dunant was a visionary humanitarian but a dismal businessman. After Solferino, he lost his business and fell into debt to friends. Instead of dining on delicacies, he had at times only a crust of bread to eat. "For years," one biographer wrote, "he lived as a beggar in misery and concealment."

THE MODERN ICRC

Over 20,000 people work for the International Committee of the Red Cross (ICRC) in Geneva and the roughly 100 countries where the ICRC is present.

Among other things, ICRC representatives work in the midst of armed conflict to teach fighters about human rights and the laws of war. The ICRC is neutral, meaning that it doesn't take sides and represents only the civilian population and prisoners of war. ICRC workers also work in prisons to confirm who is being held, advocate for their humane treatment, and help them communicate with their families.

The work remains dangerous. According to the ICRC, between 1996 and 2017, 55 staff members were killed in countries like Afghanistan, Cameroon, Nigeria, South Sudan, and Yemen.

At the end of his life, Dunant lived in a retirement home for poor people. He briefly became famous again after winning the very first Nobel Peace Prize awarded, in 1901. This prize honors humanitarian and human rights work. Since then, the ICRC has won the prize three more times, more than any other organization. In 1963, the Nobel Prize committee awarded the ICRC and the International Federation of Red Cross and Red Crescent Societies a fourth medal for their work helping the victims of natural disasters.

Despite being poor, Dunant donated his prize money to charity. He never succeeded as a banker or a businessman and never thought of himself as a great leader or hero. Yet he was a hero for refusing to stay on the sidelines and for saving millions of lives.

DISCUSSION QUESTIONS

1. For most of human history, armies haven't protected wounded soldiers or treated their injuries. Why do you think armies planned for enough weapons to fight but not for the staff and supplies needed to care for soldiers?
2. Some argue that the real problem is war itself and that war should be banned. The 1928 Treaty of Paris sought to ban war, but the treaty failed. Do you think we should try to ban war or instead work to make war less damaging to civilians?
3. Dunant believed that everyone should follow rules when they fight. What should be the punishment for those who break the rules? How could countries punish those who break the rules?

EUROPE'S CONSCIENCE:
FRIDTJOF NANSEN

🚩 **FIRST HIGH COMMISSIONER FOR REFUGEES**
👤 **1861-1930**
📍 **NORWAY**

*We are all of us explorers in
life whatever trail we follow.*

Fridtjof Nansen was an unlikely person to dedicate himself to the plight of people forced from their homes by war or famine. A polar explorer, scientist, professor, and writer, Nansen only ever went hungry or suffered the cold by choice, on his own expeditions or when he took off on one of his frequent ski trips.

From a well-to-do Norwegian family, he could have lived his entire life far from the conflict tearing Europe apart in the early 20th century. But Nansen made a different choice. He devoted the last years of his life to helping refugees, people forced to leave their homes because of conflict or disaster, like a famine. In 1921 he became the world's first high commissioner for refugees, appointed by the League of Nations, and helped save millions of lives.

Born on a farm outside modern-day Oslo, Nansen learned how to strap skis to his feet by the age of four. From then, he never stopped exploring. Nansen was robust, with ice-blue eyes and thick blond hair. As a teenager, he'd go into the forest to camp, equipped with only a coffeepot and a fishing rod.

REFUGEE

The word *refugee* comes from French and was first used to describe Protestants forced to flee France because of religious persecution in the late 1600s. The term later came to mean anyone fleeing war, violence, or natural disaster who is compelled to cross an international border.

By 2021 there were more refugees than at any other time in history. Their numbers included displaced people, who are forced to leave their homes but stay within the borders of their country.

Nansen studied zoology in college and later published research on the human nervous system. But his true love was the wilderness. In 1882 a professor urged him to join an expedition to Greenland. From a seal-hunting ship, Nansen first saw the rocky, ice-sheathed cliffs of the Arctic Circle, which he called a land of "infinite solitude. All the work of man vanishes like the track of a ship through the ice."

Several years later, Nansen began preparing to cross Greenland, which one writer described as vast snowfields broken by "a labyrinthine, ice-bound chaos of gulleys and greenish, gaping chasms among leaning pinnacles, high razorback ridges and eerie overhanging walls." Some called his plan "simple madness."

Nansen considered using skis, sled dogs, reindeer, and hot-air balloons but finally settled on wooden sleds that he and his fellow adventurers would pull. He and his crew slept in three-person reindeer-skin sleeping bags and snacked on chocolate mixed with powdered meat. When they arrived at Gothåb (now named Nuuk) on Greenland's western shore, they were emaciated and elated. Their 47-day trek became the first recorded crossing of Greenland.

Success whetted his appetite for more adventures. After commissioning his own ship, the *Fram* (Norwegian for *forward*), Nansen set out for the North Pole, hoping to be the first person to record reaching it. He planned to let the *Fram* freeze into the ice, then float with the current like a snug hotel. Realizing that the current wasn't cooperating, Nansen and a colleague left the *Fram* to set off on skis but found the ice too daunting and had to turn back.

Nevertheless, Nansen's three-year voyage made him a world-famous polar explorer. For years, he wrote books and continued his research. His fame convinced Norway to call him into diplomacy, and he helped negotiate independence from Sweden in 1905.

In 1914 he was a university professor when an assassination in Serbia helped spark World War I. In just four brutal years, fighting caused millions of deaths and displaced hundreds of thousands of people. In 1915 the Young Turks—the last leaders of the centuries-old Ottoman Empire and the new leaders of the modern nation of Turkey—began killing and forcibly expelling tens of thousands of Armenians.

The gruesome stories flooding the newspapers deeply moved Nansen. "There must be a regeneration," he once wrote his diary, "a new era with new ideals—when spiritual values will again be the end and material values only a means, when the world will no longer be ruled by mediocrity and the mob."

THE ARMENIAN GENOCIDE

Many historians consider the Armenian genocide to be the first genocide of the 20th century. Starting in 1915 Ottoman authorities killed, deported, and forcibly converted to Islam over 1.5 million Armenians. Many Armenians died of hunger and exposure in forced marches.

In part, the Ottomans did this to eliminate people who didn't share their ethnic origin. This was their way of creating a nation with a single, Turkish ethnicity. In 1923 Kemal Atatürk emerged as the first president of the new nation of Turkey.

At the time, mass killings on this scale were not considered a crime. Only after World War II was the crime of genocide established, which is the extermination of a people based on their race, religion, national identity, or ethnicity.

Nansen cheered the creation of the League of Nations in 1920, a forerunner to the UN. The league's purpose was to increase international cooperation and prevent war. In 1921 the league invited him to help repatriate Russian prisoners of war. Many had been starving in camps for years. They "have not only been through the usual deprivations and anxieties," he wrote in a league report, "but have suffered in every way imaginable, from the cold, starvation, disease, lack of care and overexertion."

Nansen believed he could help refugees. However, the league gave him no money, so Nansen and his staff partnered with groups like the International Committee of the Red Cross to send aid. By then, Henri Dunant (discussed in the chapter "The Man in White") had died, but Nansen surely knew of and agreed with his passion for protecting civilian lives. When Nansen had outfitted the *Fram*, he'd planned for every possibility. Now, his task multiplied across a devastated Europe, with hostile nations still at war.

He demanded, cajoled, and pleaded for private and government donations of funds, trains, food, clothing, and medicines. In less than two years, Nansen helped send nearly 500,000 prisoners of war from 26 different countries back home, giving the League of Nations one of its first real successes.

But there was a new challenge. The civil war following the 1917 Bolshevik Revolution in Russia meant hundreds of thousands more refugees. Many couldn't return because they faced imprisonment or execution by the new Communist regime. Nansen had to not only find a way to house, feed, and clothe families but also find countries willing to resettle them permanently.

Among them were thousands of children who had seen their families executed. Others faced centuries-long discrimination, including Jews. Once, Nansen described refugees as tennis balls, driven back and forth across borders.

Named the league's high commissioner for refugees in 1921, Nansen encountered crisis everywhere. That same year, the new leaders of the Soviet Union, formerly Russia, seized the wheat harvest, causing a massive famine. Nansen spent months trying to convince Vladimir Lenin, then the leader of the revolutionary Russian government, to let the international community help.

Nansen showed the same stubbornness that had brought him to Greenland and the North Pole. Personally, Nansen traveled to famine areas to conduct interviews and take photographs, hoping to persuade potential donors. "The famine in Russia is worse than words can describe," he wrote. "Millions of human beings are being tortured slowly to death by hunger and cold."

To the League of Nations, he argued that for the cost of a single battleship, the organization could save hundreds of thousands of lives. "In the name of humanity," he wrote, playing on their sympathy, "in the name of everything noble and sacred to us, I appeal to you who have wives and children of your own, to consider what it means to see women and children perishing of starvation."

He succeeded, helping set up over 900 feeding stations in Russia. For that, the Nobel Prize committee awarded him the Peace Prize in 1922. His work also earned him the informal title of "Europe's conscience."

In his Nobel acceptance speech, Nansen vividly described what he'd seen on his Russian journey. "I shall always remember a day in a village east of the Volga to which only one-third of its inhabitants had returned; of the remaining two-thirds, some had fled and the rest had died of starvation. Most of the animals had been slaughtered, but courage had still not been completely extinguished, and although their prospects were bleak, the people still had faith in the future." Nansen finished by calling on world leaders to prevent more war, "the greatest movement of the age."

NANSEN PASSPORT

Many refugees didn't have identity documents. Others had their citizenship eliminated by their former countries.

In 1921 Nansen supported what came to be known as the Nansen passport, the first internationally recognized legal instrument to protect refugees. About 500,000 people eventually received one, among them writer Vladimir Nabokov, composer Igor Stravinsky, and ballerina Anna Pavlova.

A new crisis emerged in 1922, as the newly formed nation of Turkey expelled tens of thousands of Greek families. Turkey's leaders had already been implicated in the century's first genocide, after they killed and sent into exile over one million Armenians, reducing the Armenian population in the region by 90 percent.

Nansen feared another mass attack, this time against Christian communities in Turkey and Muslim communities in Greece—at least two million people. Nansen helped organize an international relief effort that included a forced population exchange based on the religion of the people. Though controversial, this approach wasn't new and likely averted greater tragedy.

Although Nansen raised millions, the amounts were never enough. Some criticized him for being naive about politics. "Charity is realpolitik," he famously retorted. *Realpolitik* comes from German and means doing what's needed to serve a country's interests without worrying about questions of right or wrong.

Even as he worked to help others, Nansen, an explorer to the end, continued to write with passion about the cultures and natural world he saw during his travels. He always kept his camera at hand. To a friend, he described himself as a "son of the great woods. . . . There is the life, where I feel most at home."

At the time of his death, his tenure as high commissioner had been renewed for 10 more years. By then, Nansen had helped send tents, food, and medicines to hundreds of thousands of refugees and former prisoners. Many had been able to return home because of his work. He pioneered protection measures still in use today: international diplomacy, aid, support for return where possible, and resettlement.

After Nansen's death, a former colleague summed up his life: "Every good cause had his support. He was a fearless peacemaker, a friend of justice, an advocate always for the weak and suffering."

DISCUSSION QUESTIONS

1. Sympathy is when an observer feels sorry for another person experiencing a hardship that the observer hasn't experienced. Empathy is when an observer feels sorry for someone going through a hardship that the observer has experienced. What do you think inspired Nansen to feel sympathy for refugees undergoing hardships he'd never gone through himself? Do you need to feel empathy to take action to help others?

2. Refugees don't choose to leave their homes. They're forced to flee to save their lives and the lives of their families. Have you ever been forced to leave a home or area? How did that make you feel? Along with losing their home, what else might a refugee lose?

3. Nansen famously said, "Charity is realpolitik." *Realpolitik* refers to the morally messy business of negotiation and compromise that comes with politics. What do you think he meant? Do you agree? How do governments and groups like the UN spend money on war versus peace?

THE WHITE FLAME: EGLANTYNE JEBB

🏴 **CHILDREN'S RIGHTS CHAMPION**

👤 **1876-1928**

📍 **UNITED KINGDOM**

The only international language
in the world is a child's cry.

Sometimes, the talent that brings meaning or fame to a life isn't the one you imagine or recognize in yourself. Sometimes, it's a talent that may seem small but ends up changing the world.

That's the case with Eglantyne Jebb and her talent for publicity. Though she never wanted or even much liked children, she created the most important international effort to establish and protect children's rights in human history.

Jebb's own childhood in the English countryside was idyllic. Her family was prosperous and had a large house and servants. Jebb and her five siblings also had their extensive farm to explore. For several years, Jebb wrote a family newsletter, the *Briarland Recorder*, that featured family activities as well as her own poems, stories, and sketches. Her writing and sketching were lifelong hobbies.

Her mother instilled in her children a concern for the local poor, especially children. She often brought Eglantyne and her siblings with her to raise money for a small charity. Some frowned on women engaging in more than their husband's political work, but Jebb's mother disagreed, believing that her four children "should have work to do that should be pleasing to God."

At the time, few middle-class families allowed daughters to go to college. An aunt paid for Jebb to study at Oxford. She studied education and took a job as a public-school teacher. Middle- and upper-class English families sent their children to private schools, meaning that only working-class kids attended Jebb's school. This was the first time Jebb lived with poor people, including some of her teacher colleagues. Her poorly fed and dressed students often vanished because of illness or work obligations. They were dirty and smelled bad. In winter, there was never enough fuel to keep the classroom fire going. Jebb soon began to dread teaching, calling it "infinitely worse than breaking stones."

In her diary, she once wrote that she'd rather visit the dentist than be a teacher. She was very aware of her privilege and quit to move with her mother, now widowed. Jebb was much more comfortable doing research. Then living in the town of Cambridge, she published a study of poor local families and their needs. In 1902, she mocked the diamonds on the "very white" fingers of a Cambridge charity group and later made fun of them in an unpublished novel.

Yet her life wasn't her own. Her mother insisted that her daughter accompany her on a tour of European spas to seek treatment for Mrs. Jebb's declining health. Besides offering treatment, spas were also costly hotels where people mainly rested and dined on expensive food. While Jebb enjoyed solitude, she became increasingly frustrated with her "useless" days.

JEBB ON WAR

Eglantyne Jebb's work in her own country didn't prepare her for the vast human suffering she witnessed as a result of war. Yet she insisted that international outreach was essential even when the needs of suffering civilians seemed overwhelming. "It is in war itself, not in its victims, that the barbarity lies," she wrote.

The start of World War I in 1914 changed everything. Suddenly, the joy of fancy hotels shattered with news of the violent onslaught of Germany's army. Despite some international agreements on limiting the human cost of war—ones Henri Dunant (from the chapter "The Man in White") had helped forge—the Germans sacked cities, massacred civilians, and destroyed important sites like libraries. Among the weapons they used was poison gas.

Huge numbers of civilians fled, among them many children. Cambridge friends convinced Jebb to travel to the Balkans and tour the English-run hospitals set up for refugees, to help raise funds and awareness. This took great bravery. At the time, it was rare for women of Jebb's social class to travel alone. Once, fearing for her own life as well as the lives of local supporters, she sewed written notes of her interviews with refugees into her clothing to hide them. "The names of murdered men seemed to press against my heart till I could almost have cried out with pain," she wrote in her journal.

Along with her elder sister, Dorothy, Jebb worked to enlist support from well-known intellectuals of the time. Few expected Jebb to focus on children. She once wrote that the "Dreadful Idea of closer acquaintance [with children] never entered my head." She had love affairs with both sexes but never married or had children. Her real genius, biographer Clare Mulley writes, was to use writing and visual material, including photographs, "to catch people's imagination, enabling them both to empathize with the human issue, and believe that they could contribute personally to a meaningful solution."

Her decision to focus on children also went against many assumptions of the time, which saw childhood as little different from adulthood. Throughout Europe, children were expected to work. Governments considered them the property of their families, not individuals with specific needs and rights.

In 1919 the Jebb sisters founded the Save the Children Fund to send donations directly to groups working with Central European children. Her travels had taught her that while men often praised the glory of war, women and children were the ones who bore the brunt of the destruction and suffering. "It is the thousands of sick and starving and helpless and deserted, whose misery is unrelieved by the sense of adventure and history, who pay the price for war's arbitrament," or finality.

That April, London police arrested Jebb for handing out leaflets promoting a Save the Children meeting. The leaflets featured a photograph of a starving infant. Authorities accused her of being antiwar, a crime at the time. Jebb represented herself at trial, arguing that the leaflets promoted a humanitarian cause. Also, she asked defiantly, how could she be antiwar when the war was over? She was convicted, fined, and spent 11 days in jail.

SPIRITUALISM

Like many others during World War I, Jebb believed in Spiritualism. A movement that started in the US in 1848, Spiritualism held that human souls survived death. These spirits, or ghosts, could communicate with the living.

To open a channel of communication, believers would gather in a room with a medium, a person who claimed a special ability to summon the dead. These gatherings were called séances. Communication could be with words or sounds, such as tapping or scraping.

Other leading figures of the day, including author Arthur Conan Doyle, the creator of the Sherlock Holmes mysteries, believed in Spiritualism. Others debunked these beliefs by showing how mediums and their helpers could trick gullible Spiritualists with faked noises.

The incident taught Jebb an important lesson. Even bad publicity can help a cause. Interest in Save the Children skyrocketed. Jebb became expert at using visual images to gather support. She also used celebrities in what some derided as "stunts"—themed campaigns that drew small donations from working-class families, techniques still used in human rights and relief work today. "The world is not ungenerous," she once said, "but unimaginative and very busy." It was up to those who cared to gain peoples' attention and get them to help.

Some criticized her focus on Russian children, accusing her of sympathizing with Communists. Jebb insisted that the fund wasn't political. People from all sides supported their work. Save the Children was the first international group set up to aid children and was the first established by women. Jebb once answered a critic by saying, "I have no enemies under the age of seven."

JEBB AND NANSEN

Through her relief work, Jebb crossed paths with Fridtjof Nansen (from the chapter "Europe's Conscience"), whom she described as a "solid Viking." Like him, she resisted efforts to deny humanitarian aid based on politics. Both Jebb and Nansen were loners who felt a deep personal commitment to alleviating the suffering of others.

She would glide from the Save the Children office to the street in her somber suit, an "ethereal figure" whose famously golden hair had turned white, earning her the moniker "the White Flame." While Jebb saw much misery, she also found beauty in her extensive travels. During one trip, she marveled at the suddenness of a Balkan mountain pass. "Now we looked down, down, down ever so far below to a plain bathed in purple mists and surrounded by a great semi-circle of mountains, range upon range and up in the sky—was it clouds or was it more white peaks? My heart jumped when I saw for certain that it was indeed a further range of mountains and I doubted if I had ever seen a view so grand."

In 1922 she drafted the "Charter for Children," which argues for the right of children to have the best start in life. Jebb's charter was the basis for the Declaration on the Rights of the Child, ratified by the League of Nations in 1924.

The declaration deals with more than the effects of war. Jebb and her colleagues urged nations to limit child labor and regulate work conditions. Heads of state pledged to incorporate the principles into national laws. In France, authorities ordered every school to display the text. Long after Jebb's death, the framers of the Universal Declaration of Human Rights used her ideas to give special recognition to children as "entitled to special care and assistance."

Later, the United Nations expanded on the 1924 declaration by recognizing a child's right to a name and nationality, free primary education, and protection from all forms of neglect, cruelty, and exploitation. Over time, Save the Children expanded to include 28 member organizations, providing programs and services for children in more than 120 countries, and is currently the largest international child welfare agency.

The 1989 Convention on the Rights of the Child (CRC) was one of the first international treaties to combine civil and political rights with economic, social, and cultural rights. The CRC established under 18 as the definition of a child and was the first binding international agreement that treated children as having human rights. The CRC protects a child's right to express opinions, including in court proceedings that might affect the child, and "to seek, receive and impart information and ideas of all kinds . . . through any media of the child's choice."

Jebb died in Geneva in 1928, her health battered in part by constant travel. But her legacy continues to be enormous. Currently, the CRC is one of the most widely ratified human rights treaties in the world, meaning that countries have made it a part of their laws.

DISCUSSION QUESTIONS

1. How do you develop a sense of allyship for a group that you don't relate to or may even feel uncomfortable with? Can you think of examples in your life?

2. Why are "women and children" often grouped together? Do you think that women and children have different rights than others? What does this do to the idea that all human rights are universal?

3. Politicians, diplomats, schools, health care professionals, and families make decisions about what happens to children. Yet children rarely have a say in those decisions. Should they? Should children have the right to vote? At what age?

THE TOWERING INTELLECT: PENG CHUN (P. C.) CHANG

🏳 **DUTIES AND RIGHTS**

👤 **1892-1957**

📍 **CHINA**

Subdue people with goodness.

Peng Chun (P. C.) Chang was many things in life: playwright, musician, diplomat, theater director, translator, and dedicated educator. He was also an influential thinker behind the Universal Declaration of Human Rights. Chang was among the strongest voices in favor of separating the idea of human rights from religion or religious values.

And he fought hard for the idea that individuals had more than rights. Chang also argued that people should feel a duty to help others and make the world a better place for future generations.

Chang grew up in a turbulent period in his native China. When he was seven in 1899, the Society of the Righteous and Harmonious Fists, also known as Boxers, led an uprising against foreigners. The uprising became known as the Boxer Rebellion or Yihetuan Movement. Militants killed many and destroyed foreign-owned business and churches. The Boxers resented how foreign powers like the US and Japan forced China to give away land and accept foreign businesses that didn't operate under Chinese law. The Boxers feared that China would become just another downtrodden colony.

Thousands died, including Chinese people caught in the crossfire and foreigners. An international military force stopped the rebellion, reestablishing foreign control over China. For Chang, there was a silver lining. As compensation for damages against American business, the United States forced China to pay into a fund that sent Chinese students to American colleges. Chang was among hundreds who benefitted, arriving in the US to study for the first time in 1910.

THE BOXER REBELLION

Boxers were Chinese rebels who fought to expel foreigners from their country. English-speaking missionaries coined the term *Boxer* because the rebels intensely trained, including in martial arts.

Many Boxers were farmers who had suffered repeated drought and floods. Though the Boxer Rebellion failed, China eventually did force most foreigners to leave after Mao Zedong and the People's Liberation Army seized control in 1949.

Chang considered himself a humanist and a follower of Confucius, a Chinese philosopher born in 551 BCE. That meant that he believed in the goodness and potential of human beings, not the divine. Among other things, Confucius believed that people should treat others kindly and respect authority. Chang believed that people owed each other respect and help, ideals he later championed as a part of human rights.

"I come from the East—from the land of the Religion of Responsibility," he once wrote about his first impressions of the United States. He was dismayed by what he saw as an American focus on money above all else. "But the lands of the Religion of Greed are fast encroaching upon us."

Yet Chang was also fascinated by the vitality he saw in the arts, especially theater. His taste was exuberant and eclectic, from classics like William Shakepeare's plays and traditional Chinese opera to modern works by Norway's Henrik Ibsen. He completed a PhD in philosophy at Columbia University in 1922. For Chang, his studies not only built a better understanding about history but also began to inspire in him a vision for how to improve all societies.

After the end of China's last imperial dynasty in 1912, nationalist leader Sun Yat-sen established the Republic of China based on democratic principles. But Sun Yat-sen died of cancer in 1925, and the new nation quickly fragmented. Japan took advantage by brutally seizing Chinese territory.

Chang was tall, with an open, engaging smile. By 1925 he was a professor, shuttling between his Chinese university and America, in demand as a speaker. In the 1930s not only was China at war with Japan, but also a rebellion led by Mao Zedong threatened the government. Mao was a follower of philosopher Karl Marx and believed that China should be a Communist country led by peasants, by far the majority in the country.

In 1937 Japanese bombers attacked the city of Tientsin and specifically targeted Nankai University, where Chang taught, because of the supposedly anti-Japanese beliefs of the professors and students. Chang was well known enough to have to dress as a woman to elude soldiers as he made his way to safety.

For China's beleaguered government—fighting both Japan and Mao's Red Army—Chang was an obvious choice to represent China at the founding of the UN in 1945. Meeting in San Francisco, 50 countries came together to "save succeeding generations from the scourge of war," according to the UN Charter, and "reaffirm faith in fundamental human rights, in the dignity and worth of the human person, in the equal rights of men and women and of nations large and small and to establish conditions under which justice and respect for the obligations arising from treaties and other sources of international law can be maintained, and to promote social progress and better standards of life in larger freedom."

There was a lot of work to be done. In 1947 Eleanor Roosevelt invited Chang to tea in her New York City apartment to discuss the UN Commission on Human Rights, which would help draft of a new human rights declaration. Another guest was Charles Malik, a Lebanese philosopher, theologian, and diplomat. The two were a sharp visual contrast. The always elegant Chang—in crisply tailored suits and with impeccable manners—was an island of calm next to Malik, with his "enormous head, immense arc of a nose, burning black eyes, bristling curly black hair and bushy black eyebrows," as one associate described him.

Over tea, Chang and Malik began to debate and philosophize, a pattern that lasted until the final declaration was approved on December 10, 1948. A Greek Orthodox Christian, Malik believed human rights were rooted in religious ideas. Chang disagreed, arguing that both religious and nonreligious, or secular, ideas could inspire the declaration. Everyone should be able to embrace human rights, Chang believed, regardless of their beliefs or religious background.

MAO ZEDONG

Mao Zedong was born in China in 1893 to a prosperous farm family.

He interpreted the works of German philosopher Karl Marx in a new way that came to be known as Maoism. Reflecting China's predominately rural society, Maoism holds that farmers, not the working class, were the true leaders of Communist revolution. When his army seized control of China in 1949, it established the People's Republic of China.

One of Mao's most famous aides, Zhou Enlai, worked on theater productions with Chang at Nankai University, founded by Chang's brother. Zhou Enlai later became Mao's foreign minister and took part in the Bandung Conference along with Carlos Peña Rómulo (from the chapter "Masters of Their Fate").

Malik also argued that the declaration should be anchored explicitly in "nature." Chang disagreed, responding that different cultures should use their traditions to understand human rights. For Chang, there was never just one reality. For the declaration to be meaningful, he argued, the drafters had to go beyond any single religion or way of thinking.

MU LAN

Chang was a playwright like Chile's Víctor Jara (from the chapter "Art as Protest"). One of Chang's early works was an adaptation of *Mu Lan*, based on a sixth-century Chinese folktale about a young girl who helps repel an invasion.

Chang donated the proceeds of ticket sales to famine relief. *Mu Lan* has been adapted many times, including by Disney as an animated and live-action film.

Over the course of the afternoon, Roosevelt later wrote, the debate became so "lofty" that she resorted to simply refilling emptied teacups as the two verbally battled. To her, the lesson was not in the arguments Chang and Malik made but in the hours they spent debating. It was Roosevelt's job to actually get everyone to agree on a final human rights declaration that ordinary people could understand and believe in. Debate was important, but she needed allies who could broker agreements.

The commission chose Roosevelt to lead them as chair and Chang to help as vice-chair. Malik became the commission rapporteur, or secretary, and chaired other important committees. The vice-chairmanship gave Chang power over what was debated and for how long. Roosevelt was pleased with his skill at smoothing over disagreements. She later wrote that Chang had an "apt Chinese proverb to fit almost any occasion."

Chang fought hard to include antidiscrimination language into the many declaration drafts that circulated among the more than 140 delegates to the commission. They represented almost every country on earth. Like Carlos Peña Rómulo from the Philippines, who also helped draft the declaration, Chang believed that the delegates had to draw on ideas from many cultures, not just Western, Christian ones. Along with Roosevelt, who believed that human rights were important not just between nations but also in small communities, Chang insisted that everyday relationships in school, the workplace, and the neighborhood should reflect human rights thinking.

Chang and Malik remained adversaries. To calm tensions between them, John Humphrey, a Canadian and the newly appointed head of the Human Rights Division, drafted a 400-page document that they could whittle into something useful. Using this draft, Chang, Roosevelt, Malik, and Humphrey produced a preliminary draft of the Universal Declaration of Human Rights that could then be reviewed by the full commission.

Debate could be tedious, fascinating, or enraging, depending on the issue or the day. Representatives from countries as diverse as Saudi Arabia, the Dominican Republic, and France wrangled. The Cold War— the conflict between capitalist countries like the United States and much of Europe versus Communist countries like the Soviet Union—had already taken hold. The Soviet delegate, Alexei Pavlov, missed no opportunity to talk for hours. At one point, Malik threatened to get a stopwatch to cut off his speeches.

For Chang, despite the sometimes-tense exchanges and hundreds of separate meetings, the work was well worth it. As the declaration took final shape, Chang believed that humanity stood on the threshold of what he called a "new humanism" after the "shortsightedness" of the previous centuries.

Although Chang worked on the entire draft, he had a particular interest in Article 1, which sets the foundation for the rest of the declaration. Scholars believe that he introduced the concept of *ren*, or benevolence or sympathy for others, to the debates. This came from his long study of Confucian philosophy. What Chang meant was that people not only have rights but also live in community and have obligations to care for others. The exact translation proved difficult. Chang finally settled on the word *conscience* to reflect his meaning.

Like Malik, Chang believed passionately in Article 18, which guarantees the right to freedom of religion. Muslim states, founded on religious principles, objected, since they interpreted Islam as prohibiting Muslims from converting to another religion.

Devoted to the arts, Chang also promoted Article 27, which defines as a human right access to culture and science. Chang believed that the arts help human beings and their societies become better.

Once the declaration was adopted, Chang helped found the World Health Organization, drawing on his own experiences with disease. His first child, a daughter, had contracted meningitis and suffered brain damage.

In 1949 the People's Liberation Army (formerly the Red Army) under the command of Mao Zedong seized Beijing and established the Communist People's Republic of China. This ended Chang's diplomatic career. Defeated Chinese Nationalists fled to the island of Formosa, now Taiwan. Chang had deep reservations about both Communists and

Nationalists, since neither one seemed to value human rights or democracy. He believed in a middle way, where rights would be respected even as ills like poverty would be addressed.

Chang was never able to return to China. He settled with his family in New Jersey. To the end of his life, he remained a critic of the American pursuit of money. At the same time, Chang never doubted the importance of human rights. "In the space of just a few years," he once wrote, "years that were characterized by growing ideological polarization—a group of individuals who had themselves experienced the cruelty of war succeeded in hammering out a broad bill of rights."

DISCUSSION QUESTIONS

1. Why would the United States choose to bring Chinese students to American universities? What benefit is there to having American students at universities in China or another country?

2. How might using religion to define or inspire human rights ideas create conflict? Do all religions uphold the rights in the Universal Declaration of Human Rights?

3. Capitalist countries like the United States claim they uphold civil and political rights and freedom of expression even as many of their citizens live in poverty. Communist countries like China emphasize economic rights and claim to combat widespread poverty. What are the differences in these approaches?

EQUALITY, NOT SPECIAL STATUS: HANSA MEHTA

⚑ WOMEN'S RIGHTS ARE HUMAN RIGHTS

👤 1897-1995

📍 INDIA

Men and women are to society what the two wheels are to a chariot. Both are of equal importance.

"If there is one message that echoes forth from this conference," Hillary Rodham Clinton, then the First Lady of the United States, declared in 1995, "let it be that human rights are women's rights and women's rights are human rights, once and for all."

Clinton was speaking before the UN Fourth World Conference on Women in Beijing, China. The phrase "women's rights are human rights" made world headlines and helped mark a new global understanding. Abuses that harm women—discrimination because of gender, domestic and sexual violence, lower pay, lack of access to education, and inadequate health care, among others—were now considered human rights concerns.

Many celebrated the speech. Others glimpsed a moment of long overdue recognition for a human rights hero who had died the same

36

year. From 1947 to 1948, Hansa Mehta, India's delegate to the drafting of the Universal Declaration of Human Rights, had fought hard for women's rights.

TRANSLATIONS

Article 1 of the Declaration still contains the word *brotherhood* instead of *human beings* or *humankind*. Some delegates objected to *human beings* because of translation difficulties.

For example, the Soviet delegate argued that one proposed compromise, "all people, men and women," would not translate well into Russian. The Belgian delegate objected to what he called "the absurdity of *tons les hommes, hommes et femmes* and supported "all human beings."

Currently, the Declaration has been translated into over 500 languages, including Achuar Chicham, an Amazonian language spoken in Peru and Ecuador by about 5,000 people; Dagbani, a tribal language spoken in Ghana; Shan, an Indigenous language of Burma; and at least six separate sign languages. For example, Achuar Chicham includes the concept of "human beings" and translates Article 1 of the Universal Declaration of Human Rights as *Aints ainauti mash metek nuwanmaya akiinawaitji,* "All human beings are born free and equal in dignity and rights."

In part, she did this by standing up to another American First Lady, Eleanor Roosevelt. Mehta prevailed, establishing an important foundation for the women's rights movement for decades to come. To understand the importance of what Mehta achieved in human rights, it's important to first know more about who she was.

Mehta was born to a scholarly family in the state of Gujarat, on India's west coast. Her father, a legislator and philosophy professor, taught her that she was equal to boys. Often, he'd read aloud to Mehta and her sister, trading off between the *Ramayana*, an ancient Indian epic, and tales of Scottish chivalry written by Walter Scott, instilling in his daughter a lifelong love of books.

A hereditary prince of the region, Sayajirao Gaekwad III, also believed in women's rights. He hired an American to set up a library that was among the best in India. The librarian allowed Mehta to take charge of circulating books in her neighborhood. She loved sharing her favorites: Alexandre Dumas's *The Three Musketeers* and anything by *Last of the Mohicans* author James Fenimore Cooper.

With her sister, Mehta enrolled in Baroda College (currently the University of Baroda), where her father was a professor. Mehta was a small woman who dressed in a sari, a colorful garment commonly worn in the region. Her eyes were large and dark, with a seriousness that shines through in photographs. Baroda's male administrators and students didn't welcome women. In her memoir, Mehta remembered that the only six women in her class of dozens of men were provided a miserable living space. "Women are admitted there on sufferance. . . . We were shown to a poky little room—six by ten would be a generous estimate—called (the) Lady Students waiting room. There was no peace or privacy in this shelter, as the partition was such that we could see innumerable feet marching up and down the passage all the time."

Despite the obstacles, Mehta excelled. She continued her studies in England, where she met Indians committed to fighting for Indian independence. One was poet Sarojini Naidu, elected to lead the proindependence Indian National Congress political party in 1925. This was a "rare honour for a woman," Mehta noted. For her, this friendship "brought me out of my shell."

DIVERSITY IN INDIA

India is the world's second-most populous country. Before British rule, feudal lords known as maharajas and nabobs ruled much of the country.

India has many ethnic, religious, and language groups. While most Indians are Hindu, or belonging to the ancient religion and way of life of Hinduism, the country also has Muslim, Christian, Sikh, Buddhist, and Zoroastrian communities. Overall, Indian communities speak over a thousand languages and dialects.

Naidu introduced her to Mohandas Gandhi, the leader of India's independence movement. He believed in what he called satyagraha, or nonviolent resistance, a strategy that later inspired rights leaders like Dr. Martin Luther King Jr. in the United States and Nelson Mandela in South Africa.

Mehta returned to India and married. But even her progressive father objected to her fiancé, since he was from a lower caste. The caste system has roots in ancient India and was furthered by the British to divide Indians. In a show of support for Mehta, the region's maharaja, a kind of prince, said he would attend her wedding, lowering family tension. Later, when Mehta drafted the Indian Woman's Charter of Rights and Duties in 1946, she added language barring any "restriction to marriage on the ground of caste or community."

By then, Mehta had channeled her love of literature into her own children's books. She also translated stories into her native Gujarati, including Jonathan Swift's *Gulliver's Travels*.

As part of a countrywide strategy to oppose British rule, Gandhi focused on opposing Britain's salt tax. Since 1882 the British had barred Indians from distilling or selling their own salt. Instead, they had to buy this staple back from the British and pay a heavy tax. This was especially hard on the poor.

On March 12, 1930, Gandhi left his ashram, or religious retreat, to walk over 200 miles to the Arabian Sea in an act of nonviolent civil resistance, embodying satyagraha. He and thousands of supporters planned a symbolic act: to crystallize salt from seawater and thereby break British law. Soon, tens of thousands of people had joined him. At one stop, he asked women to mount a parallel campaign to picket foreign-owned stores. By then, Mehta had two children and worried about being arrested. Nevertheless, she organized over a thousand women to picket stores in Bombay, now called Mumbai.

Mehta's mentor, Sarojini Naidu, also protested, leading thousands to a British-run salt works. Police beat and arrested them. But the protest strategy worked. The Salt March galvanized the independence movement.

SAFFRON

Saffron, a deep orange and yellow color, is both a spice and a hue sacred to Hindus. Saffron comes from the stamen of a saffron crocus flower and is a popular seasoning for many cultures.

Indian nationalists adopted saffron as the color of their campaign. The color appears on the top third of the Indian flag.

Now well known, Mehta was offered a seat reserved for a woman on the Bombay Legislative Council in 1937. But she refused, since she opposed the idea of a special status for women. Instead, she ran and won the election. As a legislator, she advocated for better education as well as for the rights of the harijan, also called Dalit or untouchables, at that time India's lowest caste.

In public, the Indian independence movement supported women's rights. Privately, Mehta fought gender discrimination. She found humor in some daily battles. Without hesitation, legislative colleagues and staff addressed her as "sir" or "Mr. Chairman." Once, a cleaning woman whispered a blessing to her. "I could see that she was feeling very proud of her sex!" Mehta later wrote.

That support was crucial given the huge problems Mehta faced. At the time, the Indian life span was only 27 years. Many new mothers died due to lack of access to health care. Only one in four women voted. Some families forced their girls to marry as young as 10 years of age. In some communities, families forced girls into purdah, a kind of isolation, preventing them from attending school.

For Mehta, along with political rights like voting and equality before the law, Indian women needed economic rights. "In this man-made world the worth of a person is reckoned on his or her economic status," she wrote, advocating for health and childcare support, family planning, and rights to property. "It is in the economic sphere that women will have to fight hard to establish their position."

In 1946 Mehta was elected president of the All India Women's Conference, dedicated to promoting women's and children's rights. With others, she drafted the Indian Woman's Charter of Rights and Duties, stating that women were equal to men.

A year later, India won independence from Britain. As the clock ticked down the last seconds of British rule in August 1947, Mehta stood beside the leaders of the new legislature. When the clock struck midnight, Mehta presented the national flag to the legislature's new president on behalf of the women of India. "We have donned the saffron color; we have fought, suffered, and sacrificed in the cause of our country's freedom," she said. Later, Mehta and other women helped draft India's new constitution, including its provisions defending women's rights.

During that same year, 1947, India sent Mehta to the United Nations Commission on Human Rights. Mehta and Eleanor Roosevelt were the only women present who represented governments. But Mehta discovered that Roosevelt didn't agree with the importance of removing gendered language from the declaration. Instead, Roosevelt preferred words like "men" and "mankind."

To Roosevelt, Mehta explained that "the wording of 'all men' or 'should act…like brothers'" was dangerous. These phrases "might be interpreted to exclude women and were out of date." Mehta proposed "human beings" or "persons." This was especially important for Article 1, which established the idea of equality among all people.

Mehta finally convinced the commission to accept the phrase "human beings." To some, the dispute seemed minor, a matter of a few letters. But Mehta knew better. At home, she'd faced more than disagreements over wording. She'd been threatened, arrested, and beaten. She knew letters could mean the difference between "special status" and equality.

Mehta also argued that they should be planning to make the declaration a treaty, not just a statement of hopes. A treaty is a legal commitment that can be enforced, she said. Roosevelt disagreed, aware that even getting countries to agree to a declaration, or shared ideals, was a huge task. There were also world politics at play. Two superpowers, the US and the Soviet Union, wanted to block any enforcement that could lead to a world government beyond their control.

Mehta continued her advocacy for human rights after being selected as vice-chair of the UN Commission on Human Rights from 1950 to

1952. Later in life, Mehta became vice-chancellor at the university where her father had taught, the first woman to hold such a high academic post in India. Under her guidance, Baroda enrolled many more women. She also championed many improvements, including decent housing so that no student, including the women, would have to live cramped in a "poky little room."

DISCUSSION QUESTIONS

1. Colleagues and staff addressed Mehta as "sir" or "Mr. Chairman," which amused her. Why does gender in pronouns or titles matter? How would it make you feel to be addressed by a pronoun that doesn't reflect your gender identity?

2. Can you think of examples of gendered language in laws that could cause loss of rights if taken literally? Does gendered language create a second class of citizens?

3. Mehta advocated strongly for women to pursue higher education. Why would this matter? What effect would more women with advanced degrees have on society?

MASTERS OF THEIR FATE:
CARLOS PEÑA RÓMULO

🏴 **THE RIGHTS OF FORMER COLONIES**
👤 **1898-1985**
📍 **PHILIPPINES**

It is the duty of the little Davids here to fling pebbles of truth between the eyes of blustering Goliaths—and make them behave.

The Philippines is a vast archipelago consisting of thousands of islands in the Pacific Ocean. The name recognizes Spain's King Philip II, who was on the throne when Spanish adventurers established the first permanent Spanish settlement in 1565. Like the Americas and much of Africa, the Philippines became a colony—first Spanish, then American—run by foreigners who enriched themselves with the country's natural resources.

For Carlos Peña Rómulo, this history lies at the core of his commitment to human rights. He represented the Philippines at the Commission on Human Rights during the drafting of the Universal Declaration of Human Rights in 1946 and 1947. He believed colonies could use human rights as a powerful tool to free themselves. "Filipinos had invested lives and blood in human rights," he once wrote. "The Filipino people had spent close to 400 years fighting for human rights; we wanted the principles and ideals we had fought for enshrined and made secure."

45

His strong words fit his strong personality. At five feet four, he was often the smallest person in any room. Yet, as his wife later wrote, he had an infectious smile and was "utterly self-confident" and "utterly fearless," filling any room he entered. He was born the same year the United States seized the Philippines as a colony.

ARCHIPELAGO

The Philippines is an archipelago, meaning a group of nearby islands in a body of water. The Philippine archipelago stretches north to south and lies east of Vietnam.

Indonesia is the world's largest archipelago nation, with more than 18,000 islands. Other archipelago nations include Bahrain, Fiji, the Maldives, and Micronesia.

Rómulo's father, a mayor and later governor, was "bitterly anti-American" and fought the occupation. American soldiers arrested and tortured Rómulo's grandfather with what they called the "water cure," now called waterboarding. To waterboard, torturers pour water on a prisoner's face and down their throat, drowning the prisoner to the point of death.

Yet Rómulo also admired much about America, especially ideals of democracy, freedom of expression, and equality.

He described himself as a restless boy drawn to the bustle and opportunities of Manila, the country's capital. While he was still a high school student, he began writing for an American newspaper, the *Manila Times*. His salary was two streetcar tickets per day.

Rómulo—who spoke English, Spanish, and Tagalog, a Malayo-Polynesian language—quickly gained a reputation as a quick-witted, tireless reporter. His friends called him "Rommy." Rommy would spend the day in school and nights and weekends on newspaper stories and poetry. "Language has always seemed to me the most marvelous gift. Speech has been my treasure chest, and everything I have achieved in my life has been won by words."

In 1919 he left the Philippines for the first time to study for a master's degree at Columbia University. Living in New York City both thrilled and troubled him. He loved classes, parties, and the arts. But he was dismayed by American inequality and racism. Once, he invited a distinguished Filipino physician to accompany him to the Ziegfield Follies, a musical show. At intermission, an usher pulled Rómulo aside. Other patrons had complained that he had brought a Black woman to a Whites-only section of the theater. Rómulo later wrote that he hoped his guest hadn't noticed this act of prejudice because she admired America's "ideals as much as I."

Rommy had a lively sense of humor. He often told the story of how he'd traveled by train from the West Coast to New York as a poor student. To furnish his modest lodgings, he stole some small items from his Canadian Pacific Railroad sleeping berth. His fellow students began to whisper that he was fabulously wealthy. Only later did he realize that they had mistaken the CPR initials embroidered on his towels for his personal monogram.

Rómulo returned home to edit the *Philippine Herald* and advise the Philippine independence movement. As conflict gradually consumed Europe prior to World War II, his reporting focused on Asia's role in what he feared would be a world war. He was especially worried about Japan's actions to expand its empire. In 1931 Japan had invaded the northeastern Chinese region of Manchuria. This was the same conflict that forced P. C. Chang (from the chapter "The Towering Intellect") to flee his university.

Rómulo won the 1941 Pulitzer Prize for reporting on the war. His writing was prescient: on December 7, 1941, the Japanese attacked the US naval base at Pearl Harbor, bringing America into the war in the Pacific.

US Army General Douglas MacArthur commissioned Rómulo into the army to handle press relations. The work was dangerous. Suddenly, Rómulo was a top target for the Japanese. "At times I felt like a condemned prisoner in a death cell, sitting in my little room while the Japanese executioners roamed overhead," he wrote in a memoir of the war. In 1942 the Japanese Army drove the Allies from the Philippines. Rómulo fled with the US Army but had to leave behind his wife and four sons. They survived under Japanese occupation for two years. "I always say I did not enter the war; I was tossed in."

He was luckier than many. The US Army left behind thousands of soldiers and civilian employees. The Japanese Army forcibly marched them down the Bataan peninsula to camps, and thousands died.

RÓMULO AND COLONIZATION

Along with human rights, Rómulo believed deeply in independence for former colonies. These were places that European countries had forcibly occupied to extract resources to enrich themselves.

Ireland was among the first colonies seized by England. The United States also started as an English colony. Other former colonies include most of Latin America, occupied by Spain, Portugal, and the US; much of Africa, occupied by European powers; and much of Asia, occupied by European powers and the US.

One of the effects of World War II was to inspire former colonies to fight for independence, which Rómulo supported. By the time Rómulo died in 1985, only a handful of former colonies existed, including Gibraltar, held by the UK; French Guiana, held by France; and Puerto Rico, held by the US.

General MacArthur invited Rómulo to accompany him on his famous return to the Philippine Leyte Island in 1944. By the end of World War II, Rommy had earned the rank of a US Army brigadier general. Rómulo was a natural pick to represent the Philippine Commonwealth at the 1945 conference where 54 nations created the United Nations.

There, Rómulo clashed repeatedly with the Soviets, who questioned why the Philippines, not yet independent, should have a voice at all. During one heated debate, the Soviet Union delegate sneered, "You are just a little man from a little country."

Although Rómulo was fiercely committed to Philippine independence, he was also a passionate democrat and anti-Communist. "It is the duty of the little Davids here," he fired back, "to fling pebbles of truth between the eyes of blustering Goliaths—and make them behave." Always a diplomat, Rómulo later welcomed the delegate as his guest to a concert.

For Rómulo, international organizations like the United Nations were crucial for smaller countries, particularly ones still battling colonial rule. The UN gave these countries a platform and megaphone. One of Rommy's supporters was Ralph Bunche (discussed in the chapter "The Incurable Optimist"), a member of the American delegation and also a believer in independence for former colonies.

Rómulo represented the Philippines on the Commission on Human Rights from 1947 to 1948. During debates, he argued strongly for nondiscrimination, to protect the rights of people living in colonies and regardless of the "status of the country or territory to which a person belongs." As a writer, he also advocated for Article 19 and freedom of expression.

Known for his sharply tailored suits and camera-ready speeches, Rommy expressed a special affection for Eleanor Roosevelt. Like him, she could fall asleep anywhere. "I have fallen asleep in foxholes and in theaters. I can fall asleep in the midst of a sentence and waken perhaps five minutes later to carry the sentence through to its logical end," he wrote in a memoir.

THE RED SCARE

The Bandung Conference took place at the height of the Red Scare in the US, a widespread fear of Communism stoked by figures like Senator Joseph McCarthy (R-WI).

Without evidence, McCarthy and others launched fevered campaigns against government workers who he claimed were Communists and disloyal to the US government. Even a suggestion of disloyalty got thousands fired.

The entertainment industry also blacklisted thousands, among them actors, animators, composers, musicians, and screenwriters. In 1954, the US Senate voted to censure McCarthy for "inexcusable," "reprehensible," and "vulgar and insulting" conduct "unbecoming a senator." McCarthy died in 1957.

Delegates elected Rómulo as the first Asian president of the UN General Assembly in 1949. He vowed to voice "the aspirations of millions of voiceless Asians." But the Soviets held such a grudge against Rómulo that in 1953 they blocked his nomination to become the second secretary general of the United Nations, a higher position.

In 1955 Rómulo helped organize a kind of mini–United Nations in Bandung, Indonesia. The 29 Asian, African, and Middle Eastern former colonies at the gathering represented half of the earth's population. Yet many had yet to be admitted to the UN because they hadn't become independent before 1945. Unable to attend the Commission on Human

Rights meetings after World War II, some criticized human rights as the creation of colonizers, not the colonized.

But Rómulo argued that they should embrace human rights as a powerful tool against colonialism. Human rights weren't just "tape recordings from Washington or London," he wrote, copied by Asians and Africans. Together, they could create a counterweight to the great powers and speak as a unified voice for Black and brown nations.

In the United States, fearful editorials warned that the People's Republic of China, one of two Communist nations in attendance, would use Bandung to spread anti-Americanism. Chinese Prime Minister Zhou Enlai, one pundit wrote, would "employ the tactic of urbanity and suavity" to expand China's power.

But most of the delegates were, like Rómulo, strongly anti-Communist. He wanted them to believe that they were "masters of their own fate." Rómulo also warned against escaping colonialism only to fall victim to another power, whether it be Communism or authoritarianism.

The People's Republic of China initially opposed endorsing the Universal Declaration of Human Rights, in part because it had been negotiated by the former Nationalist government and P. C. Chang, not Communists. Tellingly, among the 600 delegates at Bandung, there was not a single woman, an international expression of Pauli Murray's "Jane Crow" critique of the US civil rights movement (discussed in the chapter "Imp, Crusader, Dude").

But helped by former human rights colleagues like Charles Malik, one of the delegates representing Lebanon, Rómulo and others persuaded the delegates to express support for the declaration as a "common standard of achievement for all peoples and for all nations." The statement also recognized that the declaration includes self-determination as a human right, something that was crucial to former colonies.

After Bandung, Rómulo continued writing, including a novel and a book of poetry. He served nine Philippine presidents, represented the Philippines as the ambassador to the United States, and led the University of the Philippines.

Rómulo's dedication to human rights and support for independence for former colonies remain among his greatest achievements. "At Bandung something unexpected happened," Rómulo later wrote. "The voices of freedom spoke clearly and decisively."

DISCUSSION QUESTIONS

1. Carlos Peña Rómulo sounds like a Latino name. The Philippines was a Spanish colony for about 400 years. Can you think of other countries where names have been strongly shaped by colonization?
2. The US Army commissioned Rómulo as an officer, a common practice with foreign nationals in conflict areas. What effects could this have on a military, a person, or their country?
3. In some colonies, including Puerto Rico, many residents prefer to join their former colonizers and not seek independence. What would be the reasons for choosing to become part of the United States? What would be the reasons to seek independence?

THE INCURABLE OPTIMIST: RALPH J. BUNCHE

🏴 **THE HARD WORK OF PEACE**

👤 **1903-1971**

📍 **UNITED STATES**

I have a bias that leads me to believe in the essential goodness of my fellow man; which leads me to believe that no problem of human relations is ever insoluble.

Few people suspected that Ralph J. Bunche would change the world—except his Nana.

Lucy Johnson, Bunche's grandmother, was born into an enslaved family. Many assumed she was White because of her light skin. But Nana was fiercely proud of her Black ancestry.

When Bunche was still a child, his mother, Olive, was diagnosed with tuberculosis. Nana brought Bunche's struggling family into her home in New Mexico, hoping that the dry air would cure Olive. Tragically for the family, Olive died when Bunche was 13.

Nana helped raise Bunche in Los Angeles. She believed education would help him combat the racism against Black people that permeated American life. Bunche was handsome, with a square jaw and easy smile. He excelled at school and sports—football, basketball, baseball, and track. His busy schedule was excellent preparation for his future career as a peace negotiator, creator of the first international peacekeeping force, and fierce human rights advocate.

Even though he earned the highest grades, the city of Los Angeles omitted him from a citywide honor society because of his race. Nana convinced him to keep fighting. "Naturally, my experiences with racial prejudice have never been pleasant, but I have never let any of them trouble me very much or cause me to become embittered," he later wrote.

At the University of California at Los Angeles, Bunche supported himself with an athletic scholarship and by cleaning buildings. He studied political science at Harvard, supported by money raised by his family and the Black community of Los Angeles, becoming the first African American to receive a PhD in political science.

In 1928 Bunche founded the political science department at Howard University, a historically Black college in Washington, DC. He later became the first Black president of the American Political Science Association.

At the time, news from abroad was dire. War brewed in Asia and Europe. An attempt to bring the world together in a League of Nations failed. Still, Bunche believed in the goal. One friend considered him an optimist. That wasn't because of wishful thinking but based on Bunche's hard work and "a long history of overcoming obstacles."

Bunche found segregated Washington hard to bear. When the family dog died, he tried to take it to a local pet cemetery for burial. He was told to go to the cemetery for Black people's pets.

BLACK ATHENS

Howard University was known as the "Black Athens" since so many of America's leading Black thinkers taught there. The university started as a theological seminary for the education of Black clergymen, then expanded to include liberal arts and medicine.

The name honors Union General Oliver Otis Howard, who was a founder of the university; the commissioner of the Freedmen's Bureau, created to assist formerly enslaved people; and the university's president from 1869 to 1874.

According to the university, in its first five years of operation, Howard University educated over 150,000 formerly enslaved people. Among its distinguished graduates are Pauli Murray, who faced something Bunche did not: discrimination based on gender. Others include US Supreme Court Justice Thurgood Marshall, Vice President Kamala Harris, writer Ta-Nehisi Coates, and actor Chadwick Boseman.

Bunche decided to travel to South Africa to learn about politics there. The country's official policy of apartheid separated citizens based on race and discriminated against Black people like Bunche and "coloreds," people of mixed or Asian heritage. When Bunche applied for a landing permit, he identified himself only as American. The South Africans let him in.

BUNCHE'S TRAVELS

On his travels to Europe and Africa, Bunche met the poet Langston Hughes; Paul Robeson, the opera singer and actor; and Jomo Kenyatta, the Kenyan independence leader and future prime minister. Kenyatta even tutored Bunche in Swahili.

His travels gave him deep insight into racism outside America. Bunche was especially worried about how the Nazis in Germany used race to attack minorities. The rise of fascism was not only a threat to Europe, he feared. These poisonous ideas were a threat to Black Americans, whom the Nazis considered inferior to Whites of German descent.

As war spread, Bunche made a bold decision about his career. In 1941, he accepted a job as an Africa specialist at the Office of Strategic Services, later the Central Intelligence Agency. Then he moved to the US State Department to work on building peace. He accepted an invitation to help set up the United Nations, where nations could work together to protect human rights and uphold international law. He also believed he could help end colonialism and advise new nations on independence. Bunche later described the work he did for the UN as the hardest of his life.

Bunche's intelligence, hard work, and deep knowledge brought him to the attention of the United Nations's first secretary general, Trygve Lie. A Norwegian, Lie asked Bunche to help negotiate the future of Palestine. Jews persecuted in Europe and during the Holocaust were moving to

Palestine to set up an independent state in a land they believed had been promised to them by God.

The Palestinians also dreamed of independence. The land had been part of the Ottoman Empire, which no longer existed. Britain took control of the region temporarily. After the devastation of World War II, Britain planned to leave. The challenge for Bunche was to try to find a way for Palestinians and Jews to end fighting and live in peace.

The work was exhausting and dangerous. Bunche helped set up the United Nations's first peacekeeping force to separate the warring sides. The UN worried that its planes and cars might be shot at, so Bunche ordered them painted white to symbolize neutrality, a tradition that persists to this day. There was little pleasant about the work. Bunche deeply missed his wife and children. "I talk, argue, coax, and threaten these stubborn people day and night, in the effort to reach agreement," Bunche wrote his wife, Ruth.

But Bunche managed to broker an agreement that ended the 1948 Arab-Israeli War and established what came to be known as the Green Line, which held for 18 years. For that, the Nobel Committee awarded Bunche the 1950 Peace Prize. He was the first person of color chosen for this honor.

At the award ceremony, Bunche's remarks were humble. He recognized that peace in the Middle East was far from settled. "Throughout the endless weeks of negotiations, I was bolstered by an unfailing sense of optimism. Somehow, I knew we had to succeed. I am an incurable optimist, as a matter of fact."

PING-PONG DIPLOMACY

Bunche made friends by using a technique he later perfected in his efforts to get warring groups to make peace: ferocious games of table tennis. He would invite his diplomatic colleagues to play and use the games to build personal relationships.

Bunche's matches weren't the last time that table tennis, also known as Ping-Pong, played an important role in diplomacy. At the 1971 World Table Tennis Championship in Nagoya, Japan, American player Glenn Cowan missed his bus to the competition. Chinese player Zhuang Zedong invited Cowan to ride with his team. Photographers captured the pair as they exited the bus, causing an international sensation.

Two days later, China invited the US team to travel to Beijing to play exhibition matches. Upon arrival, Zhou Enlai, the first premier of the People's Republic of China, personally greeted the nine American players. The American delegation was the first to enter China following the 1949 revolution. Called "ping-pong diplomacy," this led to normal diplomatic relations between the United States and China.

A ticker-tape parade in New York welcomed Bunche home. Los Angeles declared a Ralph Bunche Day. Bunche went on to lead peace negotiations in Yemen, Kashmir, and Cyprus, among other places.

After he retired from the United Nations, he returned to his first passion, civil rights for Black Americans. He delivered a eulogy at the 1963 funeral of assassinated Mississippi civil rights leader Medgar Evers. Bunche described Evers as a "brother, racially and in the cause of Negro liberation," using the term for Black Americans common at the time.

On the plane back to New York, Bunche wrote about civil rights as an issue with international importance:

> The question in the minds of everyone at the funeral service was the question raised by Mrs. Evers herself: 'Did Medgar Evers die in vain?' The answer, I am sure, is that he did not. It is to be found in the determination and courage being demonstrated daily by the Negro citizens of Jackson and throughout the State of Mississippi as elsewhere in the country. It is to be found in the awakening of the National Administration to the true dimension and the moral level of this problem. It is to be found also in the fact that the overwhelming majority of the peoples and governments of the entire world are deeply in sympathy with the struggle being waged by the American Negro. The answer is firm and clear that this struggle will be won.

That same year, Bunche joined the Rev. Martin Luther King Jr.'s March on Washington. He also marched with King across the Edmund Pettus Bridge in Selma, Alabama, to protest racial violence and discrimination.

At the end of his life, Bunche remained committed to the ideals Nana had instilled in him: fairness, hard work, and equality. While the world he strove to create remains incomplete, his work made real advances in peacemaking and the rights of formerly colonized and enslaved peoples. "Because I've seen so many instances of man's ability to do the right thing," he once wrote, "I see them every day. If man can do these things, he can do better things."

DISCUSSION QUESTIONS

1. Is there a difference between bias and prejudice? How would you describe the difference? Have you experienced bias or prejudice?

2. How did segregation differ in the North and South? Why were some characteristics different and others the same?

3. Bunche used table tennis to get people to let their guard down and come together. Why do you think that worked? What other low-pressure activities could bring people together to resolve disagreements?

A CASE FOR HUMANITY: BENJAMIN B. FERENCZ

▶ **THE QUEST TO END WAR**

👤 **1920–**

📍 **HUNGARY**

Law not war, that's my motto. Simple.

Benjamin B. Ferencz could never have imagined that he'd lead the biggest murder trial in human history at age 27. But that's where fate led him in 1947, with Europe still shattered after the end of World War II.

As the lead and only prosecutor on what became known as the Einsatzgruppen Trial, Ferencz found himself in charge of the fate of 24 Nazi men he intended to prove had murdered, in cold blood, more than a million people. The experience not only made him an advocate for international human rights law, he also became a passionate antiwar activist. "It's the war itself which corrupts the people whatever, whatever the nationality is," Ferencz later said. "The process of war-making turns people into murderers and they think they're heroes the more they murder."

Ferencz was born in what was then Hungary, in a thatched-roof house without running water or electricity. His father worked as a shoemaker to support his wife, their daughter, and Ferencz. As Jews, the family suffered violent attacks and persecution, including through laws barring Jews from attending school and becoming citizens. When Ferencz was only 10 months old, the family emigrated to America.

But in New York City, it was hard to make ends meet. Machines made shoes, not shoemakers like Ferencz's father. Instead, he found a job cleaning buildings. Ferencz's mother cooked for other immigrants. Ferencz earned money by delivering newspapers and working for a Chinese-owned laundry.

Soon, he added English to his native Yiddish. Always small, he was an excellent gymnast and swimmer. An uncle once told him, "You'll either be a good lawyer or a good crook" due to the frequent crime in his neighborhood. Ferencz chose law, attending the City College of New York, then Harvard University, earning a law degree.

By that time, the United States had joined Britain and France to fight World War II. Ferencz wanted to fly for the air force, but he was too short. "I couldn't reach the pedals," he later joked. Instead, the US Army assigned him to an antiaircraft artillery unit.

Soon afterward, the army offered him a transfer that changed his life. The army needed war crimes investigators. Someone noticed that Ferencz had studied the topic in law school. He eagerly accepted a transfer to the new War Crimes Unit to investigate German executions of captured Allied soldiers. This was one of the types of violence that Henri Dunant and the International Committee of the Red Cross had helped to define as a crime, through the laws of war (discussed in the chapter "The Man in White"). Every time Ferencz's unit heard about new cases, he would find a vehicle and race out to conduct interviews with witnesses, collect documents, and sometimes even dig up grave sites to identify bodies.

THE EXAMPLE OF BUCHENWALD

Ferencz was among the first Allied soldiers to enter Buchenwald, which was among the largest German concentration camps. Between 1937 and 1945, Germans sent almost 300,000 people to this single camp and killed at least 56,000 of them, among them Jews, political prisoners, Poles, Rom peoples, Communists, homosexuals, and people with mental illness and physical disabilities.

Overall, the Nazis administered hundreds of labor and death camps throughout the territories they occupied, including France, Czechoslovakia, and Poland, in addition to Germany itself. Well-known companies helped build the camps or profited from slave labor, among them the fashion label Hugo Boss, which used slave labor to manufacture military uniforms; IG Farben, which made the Zyklon B gas used to kill prisoners; and Daimler-Benz, which used slave labor to fabricate tank parts for Germany's army.

At Nuremberg, a few company leaders were lightly punished, but the companies quickly recovered. Over the following years, some did negotiate payments of reparations to victims.

But it wasn't until the Allies neared the German capital, Berlin, that Ferencz began to think more about how the Nazis treated Jews. He came across dozens of forced labor camps. From 1933 to 1939 Nazis sent political opponents to camps for supposed reeducation. Some prisoners were released, but many died of exhaustion or were killed. Starting in 1939 the Nazis permanently imprisoned supposed enemies: Polish intellectuals, Soviets, Roma, gay people, people with disabilities, and Jews, among others. Nazis executed hundreds of thousands. Hundreds of thousands more died of exposure, disease, and starvation. The Nazis dedicated six camps exclusively to the mass murder of Jewish families.

"That people could subject other people to that kind of treatment is something I will never recover from," Ferencz told one interviewer. By the time the Germans surrendered in 1945, they'd killed over 10 million people in the camps, including at least 6 million Jews.

Ferencz's work expanded from cases involving captured Allied soldiers to securing all records of mass murder. At one camp, a former prisoner eagerly greeted Ferencz and told him he'd risked his life to preserve documents. The documents contained the names of dozens of Nazi officers who'd been at the camp, essential for future prosecution.

When the war ended, Ferencz left the army and rushed home to marry his longtime love, Gertrude. But he was quickly invited back by the International Military Tribunal set up by the Allies—Great Britain, France, the Soviet Union, and the United States—to prosecute German political, military, legal, and medical leaders for war crimes and crimes against humanity.

INTERNATIONAL CRIMES

War crimes, crimes against humanity, and *crimes of aggression* are legal terms used by Allied lawyers at Nuremberg.

These crimes have a long history. The Black American journalist George Washington Williams coined the term *crimes against humanity* to describe atrocities he witnessed in the Belgian Congo. Crimes against humanity include mass killings and mutilations of the native people forced to extract rubber for European companies.

War crimes are specific to times of war and have come to mean attacks by armed fighters on civilians or on civilian locations, like hospitals and museums. Besides prosecuting Germans for war crimes in Europe, the Allies also prosecuted war crimes committed by Japanese army officers during World War II.

Polish academic and lawyer Rafael Lemkin argued for the term *genocide,* the destruction of a people based on their ethnicity, national origin, race, or religious group. The word combines of the Greek word *genos,* meaning "race" or "people," with the Latin suffix *caedo,* meaning "the act of killing."

Lemkin advocated for genocide to be included in the crimes charged at Nuremberg. He later drafted what became the 1948 Convention on the Prevention and Punishment of the Crime of Genocide, the first human rights treaty of the modern era (and older by one day than the Universal Declaration of Human Rights).

A war crimes tribunal of this size was unprecedented. Ferencz hoped the trials would demonstrate to the world that German chancellor Adolf Hitler and his top aides didn't act alone and were supported by most Germans. In Ferencz's view, these trials were "the biggest advance in international criminal law that had ever been taken to that time."

The Allies chose the city of Nuremberg to host the trials. There, the Palace of Justice building still stood despite intense Allied bombing. Also, the city had hosted the annual meeting of Hitler's Nazi Party, giving the location special meaning.

Ferencz and Gertrude returned to Germany so that he could help prosecute Nazis. He was the youngest prosecutor and one of the only Jews. In all, the Allies conducted 13 trials of Nazi officials, medical professionals, industrialists, and judges, resulting in 161 convictions. German courts later convicted hundreds more.

Ferencz and his team scoured German archives. Beneath one simple cottage, they discovered an underground cavern with 10 million Nazi Party files listing the names of anyone who'd ever joined. In innocent-seeming reports, Ferencz and his team uncovered a shocking story. The Nazis had deployed *Einsatzgruppen*, or "special units," to massacre civilians. Special units also searched out Jews and encouraged others to attack them, drawing on the history of anti-Semitism in each country.

With an adding machine, Ferencz remembered, he began to total up the official death count. "When I reached a million, I said that's enough for me." Ferencz called the evidence "a chronological listing of mass murder."

He used every argument he could to convince his commanders to let him prosecute the special unit commanders even though he'd never prosecuted a case before. So long as he argued the case alone while continuing his other work, he had their permission.

There were as many as 3,000 special unit members, a logistical nightmare for the trial. Many were dead or had escaped. The courtroom had room for only 24 defendants. Ferencz chose to prosecute 24 of the most senior and best-educated officers who were also alive and captured. Of those men, one committed suicide before the trial and another was too ill to stand trial. That left 22 defendants.

The trial began on September 15, 1947. Ferencz didn't call a single witness. He wanted the accused to implicate themselves through their own written accounts and official records. He argued for two days while the defendants took weeks to plead their innocence.

The evidence was sickening and overwhelming. One defendant directed a unit that killed 33,771 Jews in the Babi Yar ravine in the city of Kiev, in 1941. Soldiers murdered men, women, and children. As the judge later noted, the defendants ordered their deaths solely because of their religion or nationality.

The court convicted all 22 men. Among them was General Otto Ohlendorf. Ferencz proved that Ohlendorf had ordered an estimated 90,000 murders as the commander of Special Unit D of the Einsatzgruppen. After the judge sentenced Ohlendorf to death, Ferencz visited him in his cell, hoping to hear an expression of remorse. Like Ferencz, Ohlendorf was a lawyer and a father.

But Ohlendorf believed he acted under legal orders and "tried to justify what he did," Ferencz remembered. Ohlendorf was executed along with seven other defendants. The rest served prison terms.

After the Special Units trial, Ferencz dedicated himself to recovering the belongings of Jewish people that had been stolen by the Nazis, including works of art, religious objects, and hundreds of sacred Torah scrolls. He also helped negotiate restitution from the German government to the new state of Israel, founded in 1948, where many Jewish survivors settled after the war.

When he talked about his experiences, Ferencz often broke into tears. But the trauma he'd suffered also gave him purpose. All wars have atrocities, Ferencz had learned. Therefore, he decided, it wasn't enough just to have trials after wars end. He dedicated the rest of his life to ending and preventing all war.

"That was my main pitch of my Nuremberg Trial," Ferencz later said, "that humankind has a right to be protected from this kind of slaughter and abuse simply because of your race or religion."

He supported the creation of the International Criminal Court (ICC). Established by the United Nations, the ICC is the first international court set up to prosecute crimes against humanity, genocide, and war crimes. Ferencz argued fiercely to add aggression, or starting war, as a crime.

To honor his work, the court asked Ferencz to deliver the prosecutor's closing statement at its first trial, of Thomas Lubanga, a rebel leader from the Democratic Republic of Congo. Lubanga founded and led the Union of Congolese Patriots, which massacred, tortured, raped, and mutilated thousands of civilians between 1999 and 2007. The court found Lubanga guilty of war crimes and sentenced him to 14 years imprisonment, completed in 2020.

THE INTERNATIONAL CRIMINAL COURT

The ICC, located in The Hague, Netherlands, now conducts international human rights and war crimes trials. In part, this is an effort to establish justice for war crimes committed by winners and losers alike. Since the court was founded in 1998, 123 of the 193 member states of the United Nations signed the Rome Statute establishing the court, which began proceedings in 2002—33 are African nations, 19 are Asian-Pacific nations, 18 are Eastern European nations, 28 are Latin American and Caribbean nations, and 25 are Western European and other nations.

Only citizens of nations that have ratified the Rome Statute can be prosecuted by the ICC. To date, the US has refused to formally join the treaty. American opponents of the ICC fear that American officials and soldiers could be prosecuted for war crimes.

As Ferencz later wrote, during World War II, "I witnessed incredible inhumanity. I peered into the eyes of remorseless murderers—many of them men of education and intelligence. How does one cope with the complete absence of shame or regret on the part of mass killers who remain convinced that they were part of a master race and that what they did was necessary and right?"

The answer, he believed, was a determined and collective campaign to right wrongs no matter where they occurred. We ended slavery, Ferencz once pointed out. We established women's rights and tried war crimes at Nuremberg. Why not dream big to end war? "The world is filled with human suffering," he wrote, "but it is also blessed by very many people who are determined to make it a better place for all and whose individual efforts made a difference."

DISCUSSION QUESTIONS

1. The Nazis weren't the first to enslave people to work for them. Where else has forced labor been used? Is that still happening today?

2. Some people criticize the ICC for prosecuting mainly defendants from majority Black and brown countries. Who should have the power to create courts for human rights crimes? What are some of the good and bad things that might happen?

3. Ferencz said, "It's the war itself which corrupts the people whatever the nationality is." Do you agree? Can any country commit crimes during war? What happens first, corrupt intent or war? How does war start if there is no ill intent?

IMP, CRUSADER, DUDE:
PAULI MURRAY

⚑ **INTERSECTIONALITY AND HUMAN RIGHTS**

👤 **1910-1985**

📍 **UNITED STATES**

Hope is a song in a weary throat.

Pauli Murray is likely the most influential and interesting human rights hero you've never heard of. A prolific writer, lawyer, and professor, Murray developed key legal ideas behind civil rights for Black Americans and equal rights for women and lesbian, gay, bisexual, transgender, and queer people (LGBTQ) in the United States.

And she did these things well before some of the more famous activists you've learned about in school. Police arrested Murray in 1940 for refusing to sit at the back of a Virginia bus. That's 15 years before Rosa Parks was arrested in Birmingham, Alabama, for violating the same rule.

In 1948 the Methodist Church hired Murray to research the states where segregation based on race was a matter of law or simply tradition, part of its preparation for a campaign to promote civil rights. Expecting a paper, the Methodists instead received an extensive and unique study, *States' Laws on Race and Color.*

Thurgood Marshall, a prominent civil rights lawyer and later a Supreme Court justice, called the work "the Bible" for lawyers searching for ways to challenge discriminatory laws. He used it to prepare for *Brown v. Board of Education*, the case that formally ended legal school segregation in the United States.

TRANSGENDER IDENTITY

Murray may have been transgender. However, that identity was not commonly recognized during Murray's life.

In letters to family, Murray used the phrase "he/she personality" to describe herself. During her life, she used "she/her/hers" pronouns.

For this book, I'm following guidelines established by the Smithsonian Museum. The Museum recognizes that scholars and activists differ in opinion over what pronouns to use for Murray and other historical figures. In keeping with how Murray identified herself, I chose to acknowledge this history while also using the pronouns she herself used.

Yet Murray was much more than her legal work. She was an early example of living an *intersectional* life. This term was coined by law professor Kimberlé Crenshaw in the 1990s to describe how different kinds of oppression overlap. It's also come to mean how a person's race, sex, gender, class, ethnicity, and immigration status can change the way others see and treat them.

As Murray writes in her memoir, *Proud Shoes*, the violence of enslavement, rape, and segregation became a core part of her, what she calls "the degradation as well as the dignity of my ancestors."

Murray was also a gender-nonconforming person who loved women, a poet and gadfly who wrote hundreds of letters to the editor and opinion pieces, an adventurous traveler, and, at the end of her life, the first Black American woman to be ordained as a priest in the Episcopal ministry.

Her life began in tragedy. When Murray was three years old, her mother suffered a fatal brain bleed. Unable to care their six children, her father, a school administrator, sent her south to be raised by her Durham, North Carolina, family.

Murray's father also suffered from severe depression. A court committed him to an insane asylum for Black people. While there, a White guard beat him to death when Murray was only 12.

Murray moved in with her grandparents, the Fitzgeralds. They owned a two-story house in Durham's West End, a Black neighborhood. At the time, Durham was the hub of the tobacco industry and had a prosperous White and Black community.

Murray's family history was complicated. Murray's grandmother, Cornelia, boasted to her granddaughter about her White heritage but didn't like to talk about how she'd been born into slavery. Cornelia's mother, Harriet, was Black and had been enslaved. Cornelia's father was the White son of a wealthy Chapel Hill, North Carolina, family and had repeatedly raped Harriet.

In contrast, Murray's grandfather was a Northerner and Union Army veteran who'd moved south to North Carolina to teach Black children to read and write. Murray grew up in a deeply segregated society, where White and Black people rarely interacted in schools, church, and family life. Racial violence could erupt at any moment. When Murray was seven, neighbors found the body of a Black boy who'd apparently been shot for straying too close to a White man's property.

A self-described tomboy and "thin, wiry, ravenous child," Murray taught herself to read by the age of five. She started her own crusade against discrimination by walking instead of riding segregated streetcars. Her restless energy was apparent early on. She was the editor of her high school newspaper, literary society president, class secretary, debater, and both manager and forward on the girls' basketball team.

Determined to leave the South, Murray convinced her family to let her move in with a cousin in New York City. She enrolled at the all-female Hunter College in 1927, her first time in an integrated school. She later returned to North Carolina hoping to continue her studies at the same university her White ancestors had attended and financially supported. But when she applied to a graduate program at the University of North Carolina at Chapel Hill (UNC-CH) in 1938, the university rejected her based on her race.

President Franklin Delano Roosevelt had recently spoken at the campus praising UNC-CH as "representative of liberal teaching and liberal thought." Enraged by his claim that UNC-CH was progressive and forward looking, Murray wrote a fiery protest letter, making sure to copy

Eleanor Roosevelt, whom she'd met by chance years earlier. Roosevelt couldn't change the university's decision. But she maintained her friendship with Murray until her death in 1962.

DARK TESTAMENT

Murray was also a talented and prolific poet. In her poetry collection, *Dark Testament*, published in 1970, she writes about "my race and my people: the human race and just people."

The subtitle of *Proud Shoes—The Story of an American Family*—acknowledges that families come from all races, backgrounds, and economic levels. They include people who are mixed-race, like Murray. In deeply segregated America, this remains a radical message.

Barred from UNC-CH, Murray enrolled instead at the historically Black Howard University Law School with "the single-minded intention of destroying Jim Crow." There, she encountered another barrier she termed "Jane Crow": discrimination for being female. Her gender was why Harvard University rejected her application to study for an advanced law degree.

Murray never felt fully comfortable living as a woman in a world that limited what women could do, say, and achieve. She told close friends that she loved women. She rejected the term *lesbian*, instead explaining that she yearned "to be one of the men, doing things that fellows do." Even her beloved aunt perceived her gender nonconformity, calling

Murray "my little boy-girl." Today, Murray might use the term *transgender* to describe herself.

JIM CROW

Jim Crow stands for the system of racial violence, segregation, and discrimination imposed on Black people in the US after the Civil War. The term originated in the early 1800s and has been linked to a theatrical character developed by a White actor. The actor wore a costume made of rags and used burnt cork to blacken his face. He performed as a stereotypical Black enslaved person.

During Jim Crow, White violence led to the *lynchings* of thousands of Black people, a term used to describe a form of illegal execution often led and allowed by authorities. Jim Crow also meant Black people couldn't vote, obtain mortgages in White areas, travel freely, or lodge and eat in Whites-only establishments, among other things.

In her 20s, Murray explored her feelings through photographs. Well before selfies and the mobile phone were invented, Murray posed in clothing that was both feminine and masculine. She captioned one photo "The Imp," as she glances over her shoulder with a mischievous gaze. In "The Crusader," Murray wears a woman's tightly belted trench coat and skirt and carries a lawyer's briefcase and folded newspaper. "The Dude" shows Murray in masculine clothing with her short hair slicked back with shiny gel.

At the time, laws made being openly queer illegal. It was also dangerous. In later life, police detained Murray while she was dressed as a boy. A psychiatrist later misdiagnosed her with schizophrenia because she believed that she was a man. The lack of affirming and culturally competent mental health care to support her feelings of not belonging in her body was traumatic and may have contributed to lifelong mental health struggles.

In 1960 Murray briefly left America for a teaching post in Ghana. But when violence there increased, she returned home. In 1966 Murray helped found the National Organization for Women, a leading force for women's rights.

As a legal advocate and scholar as well as in her personal life, she never stopped pushing boundaries. Murray advocated for the inclusion of *sex* in Title VII of the 1964 Civil Rights Act to guarantee that Black women and other women of color would be protected from discrimination. One of Murray's many admirers was Supreme Court Justice Ruth Bader Ginsburg, also a rights champion. Ginsburg credited Murray for proposing the strategy of modeling laws to ban gender discrimination on laws banning racial discrimination. In her landmark Supreme Court brief for *Reed v. Reed* in 1971, Ginsburg argued that the Equal Protection

Clause in the 14th Amendment banned discrimination based on sex. Lawyers and activists now use that language to advocate for LGBTQ rights. As a sign of her debt to Murray, Ginsburg included Murray's name as an honorary writer of the legal brief.

In 1973 Murray left her job teaching at Brandeis University to take up a new fight, the right of women to be ordained as ministers in the Episcopal Church. She won. In 1977 she delivered her first Eucharist, or holy communion with the sharing of bread and wine, at Chapel Hill's Chapel of the Cross, where her grandmother, Cornelia, had been baptized as an enslaved child.

Murray's determination to live fully through all of her identities and embrace both the pain and the promise of the past is another gift to the human rights movement. In South Africa, the Truth and Reconciliation Commission was one tool used to build a transition from the violent segregation of apartheid to democracy. In Chile, the Museum of Memory and Human Rights both documents human rights atrocities and teaches its citizens about fundamental rights. In the US, debate over Confederate statues, the legacy of Jim Crow, and continuing inequities created by discrimination also owe much to Murray.

Murray inspired a generation of new rights activists to frame the fight for human rights through a lens of intersectionality. Her fight was never for one group. She always advocated for "my race and my people: the human race and just people."

DISCUSSION QUESTIONS

1. How do history museums present uncomfortable history? Does your city or state present a history that includes its mistakes?

2. Murray enrolled in law school as the only woman in her class with "the single-minded intention of destroying Jim Crow." Is there one injustice so great that it could compel you to choose a profession?

3. Murray was diagnosed as schizophrenic possibly because she was transgender, not because she had a mental illness. How has public perception and understanding of transgender people changed over time? How might these perceptions continue to change?

ART AS PROTEST: VÍCTOR JARA

🏴 **THE RIGHT TO LIVE IN PEACE**

👤 **1932-1973**

📍 **CHILE**

My song is not for fleeting praise
nor to gain foreign fame;
it is for this narrow country
to the very depth of the earth.

Víctor Jara believed that art was a crucial part of making positive change in Chile. Jara never thought of himself as a politician. For him, art and artists could bring people together in ways that political speeches or marches alone could not. His 1973 murder at the hands of Chile's security forces hasn't stopped his art from continuing to inspire future generations to work for human rights and the right to live in peace, the title to one of his most famous songs.

Jara is best known as a musician and singer. In the early 1970s he was one of the most prominent members of the progressive movement that elected the world's first socialist president, Salvador Allende. As Joan Jara, his wife and a professional dancer, remembered, her husband was happiest when he was traveling through Chilean villages and talking to people who thought they had no voice in politics. He had an easy manner and could sit for hours listening.

Jara was born to a poor farm family living outside Chile's capital. Like many Chileans, the Jaras were mestizo, with Indigenous Mapuche and Spanish heritage. His first memory was hearing his mother sing folk songs as she worked in their garden or cooked.

Like most farm families in Chile, the Jaras didn't own their land or house. After the Spanish Conquest of Latin America, the rich seized the vast natural resources and forced the Indigenous population to farm for them. Families would then have to pay as rent the corn, beans, and potatoes they grew, keeping for themselves only what they could raise separately along with a few chickens, a dairy cow for milk and cheese, and maybe a pig to eat on special occasions. Any money they saved was spent on what they couldn't grow, like tea or cloth to sew clothing.

Jara grew up without electricity, running water, or an indoor kitchen. Heat came from a fire burning with wood he and his three siblings gathered. The floor of the house was dirt. The children slept in a single bed.

Jara drew on his childhood memories for his songs. "The Plow" ("El Arado") describes his father's backbreaking labor. At the same time, Jara saw beauty in the natural world.

Crickets are singing
my skin gets darker and darker
and the sun glares, glares and glares
Sweat furrows me, I make furrows in the earth, on and on.

Jara's eldest sister was badly burned when a cauldron of boiling water spilled onto her. His mother moved the family to the slums of Santiago, Chile's capital, to be closer to hospitals. By then, his father had largely abandoned the family, so his mother cooked and sold street food to support them.

THE CHILEAN ECONOMY

Prior to 1970 Chile's economy depended on the foreign companies that extracted its abundant natural resources. Salvador Allende, a physician, believed Chile should control its own wealth. The United States perceived that as a threat to its national interests and the interests of US-based corporations.

As it had in Iran, the US supported the 1973 coup by Chile's military. For decades, US officials downplayed or excused the dictatorship's massive human rights violations. The dictatorship tortured and illegally detained an estimated 40,000 Chileans between 1973 and 1990, with thousands more executed. Many families still search for their loved ones.

She rarely sang anymore. But she'd propped her guitar in a corner. A neighbor offered to teach Jara how to play. He plunked out tunes he remembered her singing and scribbled down poems to match the notes.

When Jara was 15, his mother died suddenly. Thinking he'd become a priest, he enrolled in seminary school and learned Gregorian chants. But he soon realized that he wasn't a good fit for the priesthood. After completing his obligatory military service, he enrolled in the University of Chile's theater school and began to direct plays. He was the only poor student there, but he knew he'd found his place with other artists. People remembered his intense brown eyes and shock of thick, black hair.

In the 1960s a growing progressive movement challenged Chile's wealthy families and the multinational companies that controlled the country's politics as well as lucrative natural resources in copper, hydropower, and timber. The Jaras were well aware of America's military interventions in Iran, Cuba, and Guatemala and feared a similar fate for Chile.

At the same time, artists like Violeta Parra, also a musician, were rediscovering the richness of Chile's Indigenous and mestizo culture. Parra and her two children, Angel and Isabel, were part of a movement known as *nueva canción*, or new song, a melding of folk tradition with new lyrics and tunes. Rejecting pop-star costumes and electric instruments, Parra dressed and sang as a peasant, with a voice that one listener said seemed to "grow out of the earth."

Jara started recording his songs. He performed throughout South America, often dancing a traditional Chilean folk dance, the *cueca*, his feet stamping and his hand swirling a handkerchief. He and others started performing at marches and protests, their music a soundtrack to the rising demand for political power for the poor and working class.

The Parra family opened a music club dedicated to *nueva canción* as well as original art, including weavings. One night, the crowd urged Jara to sing. The applause was thunderous. People began to talk about a new singing star.

Jara continued to work in theater even as his music career took off. Some friends tried to talk him into doing charity work, but he bristled. Food, housing, education, and jobs were rights, not things that should rely on someone else's charity. "You have the right to somewhere decent to live, to a doctor within reach when you are ill, to a good education for your children! What's the use of a lampshade if you have no house to put it in?"

He wrote furiously, his songs like short stories. Jara believed music gave voice to the poor and shone a light on society's injustice. To one journalist, he said,

> I am moved more and more by what I see around me, the poverty of my own country, of Latin America. . . . But I have also seen what love can do, what real liberty can do, what the strength of a man who is happy can achieve. Because of all this, and because above all I desire peace, I need the wood and strings of my guitar to give vent to sadness or happiness, some verse which opens up the heart like a wound, some line which helps us all to turn from inside ourselves to look out and see the world with new eyes.

Jara helped found two *nueva canción* bands, Quilapayún and Inti-Illimani. Both played with guitars and native instruments like the *zampoña*, or pan pipe, and the *bombo* drum.

Chileans loved his album *La Población*, translated as "The Neighborhood." Jara wrote the songs based on interviews he conducted with the residents of Herminda de la Victoria, a housing project built on wasteland in Santiago. By then, he was a professor at the State Technical University. Often, he'd be singing at a rally when police would start arresting and beating the audience. One of Jara's songs, "Móvil Oil Special," became an anti-American anthem, denouncing the US-based Mobile Oil company and supporting student protest.

QUILAPAYÚN AND INTI ILLIMANI

Quilapayún is a Mapudungun word. Mapudungun is the language of South America's Mapuche people. The word means "three bearded men"—describing the group's original founders.

Inti-Illimani comes from two South American languages. *Inti* is Quechua, the language of the Inca empire that is still spoken through the Andes. The word means "sun." *Illimani*, from the related Aymara language, is the name of a 21,000-foot peak in the Bolivian Andes.

Joan Jara became increasingly afraid for him and their two daughters. Once, as Jara emerged from the university, she saw a group of wealthy-looking students surround Victor, shouting. Jara later told her that they "had threatened that they would 'get him' if he persisted in singing subversive songs."

But Jara never wavered. "There was no doubt that his commitment and his resolve were strengthened rather than weakened by it," Joan Jara later wrote. "He took a step forward rather than backwards in the face of violence, taking the risk with his eyes open."

In 1969 a human being was about to step on the moon. But in Chile, all eyes were on the 1970 presidential election. Some Chileans, inspired by revolutionary movements in Cuba and Colombia, took up arms. In response, right-wing militants began attacking organized workers and farmers.

A SEARCH FOR THE KILLERS

For years, the Jara family searched for the identity of his killers. In 2018 a Chilean court sentenced eight retired Chilean military officers to 15 years in prison each for his murder. A ninth suspect was jailed for five years for his role in covering up the killings.

In 2016, a US civil court jury found a US citizen and former Chilean military official liable for torturing and killing Jara. To date, the United States has refused to return the officer to Chile for trial.

But support for Salvador Allende proved decisive. He was inaugurated on November 3, 1970. His political alliance, Popular Unity, moved to nationalize the copper mines and banks and guarantee medical care and housing. Every poor child, Allende promised, would have a glass of milk a day to combat hunger.

At night, the telephone in the Jaras' home rang constantly with threatening calls. Yet the family believed that Chile's long tradition of democracy would stand against dictatorship.

The Jaras weren't prepared when General Augusto Pinochet ordered Chile's air force to bomb the presidential palace on September 11, 1973. As news of a military takeover spread, Jara left home to join his colleagues at the university. Later, police detained Jara and hundreds of professors and students and herded them into the city's National Stadium, where Jara had once played for adoring crowds.

An officer recognized him and began to beat him, especially the hands he used to play his guitar. Despite the abuse, witnesses remember Jara singing a famous political song of the time, "Venceremos" ("We Will Win").

At one point, Jara asked a fellow detainee for a pen and paper to write what would be his last poem, "Estadio Chile."

> *How hard it is to sing when I must sing of horror*
> *Horror which I am living, horror which I am dying.*

Days later, Joan Jara collected Jara's body from the morgue. Jara was 40 years old. She considered herself among the lucky ones. Many families never received any information about their loved ones' fate or whereabouts. In case after case, Chile's military, police, and intelligence services tortured and killed detainees, burying them in mass graves or dropping their bodies into the Pacific Ocean.

Jara's music and his example continue to inspire Chileans. In protests, Jara's music is still part of the soundtrack. Every year, thousands of guitarists gather in Santiago and around the country for the thousand-guitars tribute. The lyrics to his "Manifiesto" remain as relevant as ever.

My guitar is not for the rich
no, nothing like that.
My song is of the ladder
we are building to reach the stars.

DISCUSSION QUESTIONS

1. Can you think of a song that has lyrics about creating positive change in the world? Is there a protest song that has a special meaning for you?

2. Víctor Jara wrote, "You have a right to somewhere decent to live, to a doctor within reach when you are ill, to a good education for your children!" One of his famous songs declared a right to live in peace. Do you agree that these are or should be human rights? How can we defend these rights?

3. The act of a nation taking control of its own natural resources—and removing control from more powerful nations or multinational corporations—links the stories of Jara, Iran's Shirin Ebadi (from the chapter "The Tightrope Walker"), the Philippines's Carlos Peña Rómulo ("Masters of Their Fate"), and Honduras's Berta Cáceres ("Sacred Rivers"). Why would this be so linked to human rights?

DETERMINATION, PATIENCE, INSISTENCE: JUAN E. MÉNDEZ

⚑ ENDING TORTURE

👤 1944–

📍 ARGENTINA

Human rights work is about change.

When he speaks about the torture he suffered at the hands of Argentina's police in 1975, Juan E. Méndez is matter-of-fact. Arrested for his work as a lawyer, he was beaten, shocked with an electric prod, threatened with execution, and told that his wife and young sons would be tortured in front of him.

"Needless to say, I screamed at the top of my lungs," he later remembered about the abuse. "The interrogators assured me that no one could hear me." His only solace was knowing that he wasn't giving his torturers information that would help them detain and torture others.

Defending others is how Méndez started his long career in human rights. He sustained his commitment through a fierce combination of the quietest strategies possible: determination, patience, and insistence.

Argentina is the world's largest Spanish-speaking nation, with a long Atlantic Ocean coastline and immense plains, the Pampas, bordered to the west by the Andes. Méndez grew up in Mar del Plata, a resort town south of the capital of Buenos Aires. Like many in this soccer-mad country, as a boy he was a big fan of professional soccer teams.

Méndez has the compact build of a soccer player. He also exudes a kind of calm that could have lulled an opponent into overlooking his passion. But it was his passion for justice that led him into the courtroom.

He began practicing and teaching law during a turbulent time. Argentina was split between the wealthy and middle class on one side and the much more numerous working poor on the other. Juan Domingo Perón, a former army colonel, won the 1946 presidential election largely on the votes of the poor, often called the *descamisados* or "shirtless ones."

As he'd promised, Perón nationalized the banks, factories, and railways; raised wages; and created the county's first social welfare system. Soon, the government controlled virtually every aspect of Argentina's economic life. Perón wanted Argentina to be self-sufficient, so he heavily taxed imports while providing subsidies to Argentine businesses.

His decisions made prices skyrocket, putting food and other necessities out of reach for many. Protesters clogged the streets and the square in front of the presidential palace in the capital, Buenos Aires. The police retaliated, beating and arresting thousands.

Argentina's military finally ousted Perón in 1955 and banned his political party. While Méndez still dreamed of a soccer career, Perón left for exile in Spain.

But the unrest continued. In 1973, the Peronista movement, under the Justicialist Party, forced the then-president to resign, prompting new elections and Perón's dramatic return to Argentina to retake the presidency. His second wife, Isabel, served as vice president. By that point, the Peronista coalition of workers, left-wing students, and the security forces fractured. People fought openly in the streets. Added to the mix was a newly formed rebel army, called the Montoneros, inspired by Argentina's independence wars in the 1800s.

By 1974 Méndez, a lawyer and law professor, was the advocate students, workers, and Perón's political opponents turned to when they were arrested. His work made him a target. One day in 1974, when he was leaving the classroom, security force officers grabbed him. "Dozens of people were passing by," he later wrote. "It all happened out in the open, as if it were something ordinary."

Students immediately notified his wife, Silvia, also a lawyer. She alerted family and colleagues. A crucial way to ensure the safety of a detainee was to file a writ of habeas corpus, a Latin phrase for a law compelling the authorities to confirm that a person is in custody. This helps prevent a "disappearance," when authorities hold someone secretly and often torture and kill them, a practice the Argentine government used frequently in the 1970s.

Police released Méndez after three days. But he and Silvia knew their family wasn't safe anymore in Mar del Plata. They moved to Buenos Aires to continue their legal work. Perón died in 1974, making Isabel president, the first woman in Argentina's history to achieve that office. But her policies only increased violence. Her government helped create the Argentine Anticommunist Alliance, which killed hundreds of government critics, among them the priest who baptized Méndez's two children.

Four months after her husband's death, Perón declared a state of siege, suspending constitutional rights such as the right to assemble and travel freely. This also gave police greater powers to arrest. Méndez remembered how a sense of violence hung in the air, with police and armored vehicles everywhere. "But the real terror, the kind that kept you up at night, was the realization that regular or irregular forces could kidnap you at any moment and not suffer any consequences. If you were meeting a political friend or a client at a café, you had to make sure no one had followed you or your friend, and then you had to keep a constant watch on the door."

In August 1975 plainclothes police again snatched Méndez off the street. For two days, police savagely tortured him, pausing only to allow the interrogator to ask more questions. "More than once, I begged my torturers to kill me," he wrote in his memoir, *Taking a Stand*. "They said they would, but later. Years later I think about it and wonder if I really meant it. I think I did, at the time."

EVITA

Many know Juan Domingo Perón through his first wife, María Eva Duarte de Perón, whom Argentines called Evita. A stage performer with her own political aspirations, Evita championed women's suffrage during her husband's first presidency.

Juan Perón appointed her to head the country's Ministries of Labor and Health. She also established her own charitable foundation and the nation's first major female political party, the Female Peronist Party. She died of cancer in 1952.

The next 18 months of prison were "utter desolation" for him, separated from his family and unable to help others. But he knew that people from around the world were demanding his release. That left a powerful impression on him. Even in his cell, he wasn't forgotten. Among the people was the Iowa family who had hosted him as a foreign exchange student in high school. Amnesty International, a leading human rights group, adopted him as their first Argentine "prisoner of conscience," a term that means someone who advocates peacefully for change.

For Méndez, this opened a new way of understanding human rights. "Mine was an isolated case," he later wrote, "but it also shows that determination, patience, and insistence by common men and women can produce results in the struggle for justice."

Supported by the United States, the Argentine military deposed Isabel Perón in a coup, then began a campaign to force its ultra-conservative, Catholic, and anti-Communist views on the country. Between 1976 and 1983, Argentina's security forces "disappeared" an estimated 30,000 people, targeting unionists, students, and political activists.

Human rights advocates put the word in quotations because these people don't literally vanish. A "disappearance" is when the government seizes someone but doesn't record their arrest or even inform their family. Often, "the disappeared" are interrogated, tortured, then killed.

ACCOUNTABILITY

Latin American dictatorships "disappeared" tens of thousands of people in the second half of the 20th century. In both Argentina and Chile, some "disappeared" people were drugged, then flown over the ocean where they were dropped and drowned.

Méndez was able to identify the men who tortured him. They were later prosecuted, found guilty, and sentenced to jail terms. Argentinian human rights groups say that many of those who tortured, "disappeared," and killed during the dirty war have since been prosecuted and punished.

Throughout Argentina, officers dressed in street clothes would snatch people from workplaces, schools, and homes. Many were later killed, their bodies dumped into the ocean or buried in mass graves. Young women who were pregnant at the time of their "disappearance" gave birth in custody, then were killed. Officers would secretly send the infants to military and government-allied families for adoption.

Méndez considers himself lucky. He was released in 1976 and sent into exile with his family. For him, though, his battle for human rights had just begun. Just as he'd refused to stop helping people as a young lawyer, he knew that his experiences as a political prisoner and torture survivor gave him a powerful platform to help others.

In America, Méndez met the human rights activists who'd set up Helsinki Watch, a nongovernmental organization meant to document rights abuses in Europe. They thought it was time to start a new group to work on human rights in Latin America. In 1982 Méndez became the first director of Américas Watch, now a part of Human Rights Watch, the largest US-based human rights advocacy group.

AMNESTY INTERNATIONAL

Amnesty International (AI), a human rights nongovernmental organization with tens of thousands of volunteer members from across the world, formed in 1961. Groups of volunteers "adopt" prisoners of conscience and work for their release by writing letters to governments and publicizing the injustice.

According to their definition, a prisoner of conscience is someone "who is physically restrained (by imprisonment or otherwise) from expressing (in any form of words or symbols) an opinion which he honestly holds and which does not advocate or condone personal violence." AI won the Nobel Peace Prize in 1977.

He saw the Argentinian model of "disappearing" and torturing people repeated throughout Central America. One case that caught his attention involved the "disappearance" of Angel Manfredo Velásquez Rodríguez, a Honduran economics student. Méndez helped bring the case to the Inter-American Court of Human Rights, a regional body formed to uphold human rights in the Americas. Now known as *Velásquez Rodríguez v. Honduras*, the case broke new legal ground by finding Honduras guilty of crimes against humanity for "disappearances."

This was the first time a court obligated a nation to investigate, prosecute, and punish those responsible for the crime of "disappearance."

In 2004 Méndez took on two new challenges: the directorship of the International Center for Transitional Justice, which encourages countries to form truth commissions to face up to their violent pasts; and the role of first special adviser on the prevention of genocide to the UN secretary general, Kofi Annan. That brought a new urgency to his work, as he would not just respond to atrocity but also try to prevent it.

Méndez helped set up an early-warning system to inform world leaders when and where they could take measures to prevent genocide. The work was difficult and largely thankless. It's difficult to celebrate the absence of abuses. Méndez believed the international community needs to do much more to prevent abuses, not just respond to them once they happen.

True to his commitment to remaining determined, patient, and insistent, Méndez accepted an appointment as the UN special rapporteur (an independent expert who monitors, advises, and publicly reports on human rights in specific countries or on specific themes) on torture in 2010, a post he held for six years. The work brought him full circle. One of his principal responsibilities was addressing the United States' unjustified and illegal use of torture after the September 11, 2001, attacks on New York and Washington, DC. Not only is torture ineffective, he often said, but also "torture only breeds more crime and more terrorism."

Again and again, Méndez uses the word *patience* when describing his approach to human rights. He endured torture without giving up hope. In conflicts around the world, he insists on staying with negotiations until they succeed. While still serving as the UN special rapporteur on torture, Méndez successfully appealed to the UN General Assembly to develop standards to guide information gathering, without torture, by government officials, like police. In his honor, the guidelines are called the Méndez Principles.

Méndez says that he considers himself privileged to engage in the work of human rights. "The only weapons of the human rights movement are words and peaceful political action; that is precisely why we fight with the arms of reason. We will win not so much if we win the debates but if we persuade and convince."

DISCUSSION QUESTIONS

1. Despite much evidence demonstrating that torture doesn't work, it's still commonly used. Why do you think that's true? What arguments might be used to persuade people not to torture others?

2. For a time, Méndez worked on a system that might prevent genocide from starting. What do you think are signs that genocide is starting to happen? What historical examples can you think of?

3. Méndez says that "torture only breeds more crime and more terrorism." Do you agree? If so, why do you think this is true?

THE TIGHTROPE WALKER:
SHIRIN EBADI

🏴 **ISLAM, IRAN, AND HUMAN RIGHTS**

👤 **1947–**

📍 **IRAN**

Everyone who has a throat to shout with and a pen to write with should say "enough."

Shirin Ebadi is tiny, with a thick cap of dark hair. She often uses a stepping stool so that audiences can see her from behind a lectern.

Once she starts speaking, though, every eye is riveted. It's not just her sense of humor or deep knowledge of law, literature, and history. Prominent Iranian faith leaders oppose human rights, especially for gay people and women. These beliefs are also embraced by Iran's current leaders, who have persecuted Ebadi and other human rights advocates. Ebadi calls herself a "tightrope walker" for claiming human rights as a faithful Muslim and an Iranian citizen. Her fierce commitment led to international prominence and the first Nobel Peace Prize for a Muslim woman and Iranian, in 2003.

Speaking the truth no matter who objects or the dangers the truth may cause for her is as vital to Ebadi as air or water. Every human being, she believes, must "illuminate the dark spots where dictators hide. This is the duty of each and every one of us who believes in the future of humanity."

One of Ebadi's first memories was at her family's spacious home west of Iran's capital of Tehran. Her usually indulgent grandmother snapped at her and the other grandchildren on a warm August night in 1953, the radio humming in the background.

Still a small child, she didn't realize that her grandmother was listening to the news. With the support of Iran's military, the shah, or king, of Iran had just deposed the democratically elected prime minister and parliament. Angered by the prime minister's decision to nationalize the country's oil reserves, the United States helped plan the overthrow. At the time, Iran was a major oil producer for the US and Britain.

Iran is a patriarchal society, with men in most positions of influence. But Ebadi's family raised her to think of herself as equal to her brother. She also grew up with a strong sense of justice no matter the cost. "Whenever I would see children fighting, I would naturally try to defend the underdog, the weakest," she writes about herself. "I even got beaten up myself a couple of times doing that!"

When she was a college student, many younger women students chose not to wear the hijab, or veil. The shah banned the veil in an effort to modernize Iran. He promoted women to positions of influence and power even as his feared intelligence agency, SAVAK, imprisoned, tortured, and killed his opponents and prodemocracy supporters.

Ebadi started studying law in 1965. Five years later, at only age 23, the Justice Ministry appointed her to serve as one of the country's first women judges. At the time, opposition to the shah was growing. Along with Ebadi, many Iranians saw hope in the fiery anti-shah speeches of Ayatollah Ruhollah Khomeini, a Shia cleric.

US INTERVENTION

The US-backed overthrow of Iran's democracy in 1953 became a model deployed repeatedly to end democratically elected governments. American presidents of both parties feared leaders who opposed US policies, especially if those leaders were socialists or questioned capitalism and the power of multinational corporations.

Funneling funds through the CIA, the US paid Iranians to protest and newspaper editors to publish stories critical of the prime minister. Similar techniques were later used against democratically elected presidents of Guatemala, the Republic of Congo, and Chile, among others.

Like most Iranians, Ebadi is Shia, the world's second largest Muslim group. The largest is Sunni, whose followers share some fundamental beliefs and practices with Shia. However, the two groups differ on who became the leader of Islam after the death of the founder and Prophet Muhammad. As Ebadi writes in her memoir, *Iran Awakening*, about Ayatollah Khomeini, she felt more sympathy for this seemingly humble cleric than the champagne-loving shah, famous for partying with American starlets.

Ayatollah Khomeini's coalition included prodemocracy activists, Marxists, nationalists, and socialists. "It did not seem so alarming that mullahs should take the lead," she noted, using the term for a lower-level cleric. Huge protests led to the shah's departure from the country in 1979. Ayatollah Khomeini took control, soon afterward declaring an Islamic Republic.

MUSLIM CLERICS

Ayatollah is the Shia term for a high-ranking cleric. Sunnis use the term *mufti*. In Shia Islam, a lesser cleric is a mullah. Both Sunni and Shia use *imam* to mean someone holding a religious leadership position.

Among Muslims, women can wear different coverings either by choice or force. The hijab, or hejab, covers the hair, neck, and shoulders. The chador, common in Iran, includes a head covering and cloak that reaches to the feet. The niqab is like a chador but has an element that also covers a woman's mouth and nose. The burka, or burqa, covers the entire body and includes a mesh panel over the face.

For a brief period, Ebadi felt hopeful. But her first warning that things would take a dangerous turn happened at work, when her new supervisor told her and other female employees to cover their hair. "Here we were, in the Ministry of Justice, after a great popular revolt had replaced an antique monarchy with a modern republic," she wrote in her memoir, "and the new overseer of justice was talking about hair. Hair!"

Like China's P. C. Chang (from the chapter "The Towering Intellect"), a Buddhist, and India's Hansa Mehta ("Equality, Not Special Status"), a Hindu, both drafters of the Universal Declaration of Human Rights, Ebadi believes that human rights are compatible with all religions, including Islam. "Human rights is a universal standard," she insists. "It is a component of every religion and every civilization."

In November 1979 a group of college students loyal to Ayatollah Khomeini seized the US embassy in Tehran along with 52 American hostages. In retaliation, the US imposed heavy sanctions, banning most exports to Iran. Although the hostage crisis ended after 444 days, tensions only increased as the increasingly hardline Iranian government sent loyalists to places like Lebanon and the Palestinian Gaza Strip to spread their militant interpretation of Islam. In 1983, pro-Iranian fighters bombed a US military base in Beirut, killing 241 US Marines.

That same year, the Islamic Republic stripped Ebadi and other women of their judgeships for being women. With growing dread, she read law after law imposed by the new Islamic government. The regime assessed the value of a woman's life and her testimony in court as half that of a man's. A woman had to ask her husband's permission to divorce. "The laws, in short, turned the clock back fourteen hundred years," she later wrote, "[to] the days when stoning women for adultery and chopping off the hands of thieves were considered appropriate sentences."

Some friends fled Iran. Others vanished into prison. Horrifying stories circulated about torture and executions. Just owning supposedly subversive books could get a person and their family killed. The government refused to approve Ebadi's license to practice law, so she instead taught law and wrote books and articles.

In 1980 Iraq invaded Iran, taking advantage of the turmoil. The war included appalling abuses. Iraq intentionally targeted civilians, sometimes with illegal chemical weapons. Iran made young men into human shields; they died in wave after wave of infantry attacks. When a truce ended hostilities in 1988, over 500,000 soldiers and at least 100,000 civilians were dead on both sides, with no side gaining any territory or advantage.

IRAN AND NUCLEAR WEAPONS

Iran launched a nuclear weapons program in the 1950s. In 2015 Iran, the United States, and other countries signed an agreement that limited Iran's development of nuclear weapons.

The US withdrew from the agreement in 2018. Iran then resumed its nuclear-enrichment program.

Ayatollah Khomeini died in 1989. Ebadi allowed herself to hope that democracy would again return. Then married with two daughters, she successfully reapplied for her law license and began taking on high profile human rights cases.

But instead of a return to democracy, Iran became even more extreme. Ebadi believes a "clique of revolutionaries" took power and immediately cracked down on dissent. Morality police, called *komitehs*, targeted women specifically for the smallest supposed offense, like wearing makeup. Despite their stated goals of protecting the family, women, and children, Ebadi uncovered case after case of shocking state-sponsored abuse. "Islamic law tore children away from mothers in the case of divorce, or made polygamy as convenient as a second mortgage," she wrote.

In one case, she represented the mother of a nine-year-old girl beaten to death by her father and half-brother. The mother had divorced the girl's father to escape his drug use. Yet because a woman has fewer legally recognized rights, a court granted custody to the abusive father. The father was acquitted of murder and the half-brother received only a two-year sentence. Although Ebadi was disappointed, the case did lead to a reform that allows mothers to gain custody when fathers are deemed unfit.

Ebadi believed women have always been key to Iran's democratic future. Currently, over 65 percent of university students are female. Other Islamic states, among them Bahrain and the United Arab Emirates, have women as cabinet-level ministers.

The region-wide "culture of patriarchy" has to change, she believes. Women should be free to follow their dreams, and that means being able to leave their homes without fear of being arrested for the wrong clothing or no head covering. "There is a popular saying that modernity is born in the street," she once wrote. "A woman who comes to the street cannot go back to the old traditions. And this was the key to the freedom of Iranian women."

In 1999, while reading through legal materials, she saw her own name listed as a government target for attack. The document included a caution: government killers should wait until after the Muslim holy month of Ramadan, when many Muslims fast, even though the clerics considered Ebadi an "infidel," or nonbeliever.

Later, the government arrested and tortured Ebadi for her legal work. For her, the problem isn't Islam but how the religion has been interpreted as part of a patriarchy that has a long history of violence against women. "It was through this belief—that the intellectuals, that I, had abandoned God—that they justified the killings as a religious duty," Ebadi explains in her memoir. "In the grisly terminology of those who interpret Islam violently, our blood was considered halal [or allowed], its spilling permitted by God."

The regime canceled her law license in June 2000, then detained her and kept her in solitary confinement for 25 days. The next year, Ebadi helped establish the Defenders of Human Rights Center to defend human rights and provide free legal services.

At the ceremony for her 2003 Nobel Peace Prize, she dedicated the award to the Iranian people. "This award sends out various messages, that Islam is not a religion of terror and violence and that the world community supports the struggle of Muslim women for freedom and justice. Personally, I feel it belongs to the Iranian people and those who work for human rights and democracy."

After a wave of new prodemocracy protests in 2009, Iranian police broke into Ebadi's Tehran apartment, beat her husband, and confiscated the Nobel Prize statuette. Traveling at the time, she has since lived in exile. Yet she continues to advocate not only for Iran, but for human rights and peace around the world. In 2020, she dedicated especially strong words to the United States for breaking its commitment to a treaty with Iran to end its development of nuclear weapons.

Ebadi remains hopeful about Iran because young women lead most protests. She believes that human rights activists like herself "do not have the right to lose hope." If a boat is sinking, she asks, "is there any other way but to swim? If one becomes tired and discontinues swimming, that person will sink. We have to be hopeful."

DISCUSSION QUESTIONS

1. If a movement you supported gradually changed its goals away from ones you shared, would you still support it to be loyal? Or would you seek a different way to support your goals?
2. Persecuting human rights activists isn't unique to Islam or the Middle East. Can you think of other examples of religions or cultures targeting rights advocates?
3. Ebadi believes that human rights can be a part of any religion. Do you agree? What can believers do to support human rights?

REFUSING TO BE SILENT:
JUDITH HEUMANN

⚑ THE DISABILITY RIGHTS MOVEMENT

👤 1947–

📍 UNITED STATES

*It is not a tragedy to me that
I am a wheelchair rider.*

"Implement Section 504" doesn't sound like a stirring call to action. But without people like Judith Heumann and the disability rights movement pushing for this obscure government rule, we might not have buildings with ramps and doors accessible to people in wheelchairs—or closed captioning for television shows, services for people with learning disabilities, or funding for personal assistants to help disabled people dress or shower. Disabled people would still be invisible and without full human rights.

Born in Brooklyn in 1947, Heumann contracted polio as an 18-month-old. Polio is a virus that can infect the spinal cord. That year, doctors diagnosed nearly 43,000 American children with polio. Some, like Heumann, became permanently paralyzed.

The pediatrician told Judy's parents to place her in a special institution for people with physical and mental disabilities. At the time, these institutions were notorious. Staff often left children and adults naked and unwashed. There were many documented cases of physical abuse, including rape, as well as unauthorized medical experiments conducted on residents.

POLIO AND PUBLIC SERVICE

The polio virus had existed for centuries before scientists developed a vaccine in the 1950s.

Among the more well-known survivors was Franklin Delano Roosevelt, president of the United States from 1933 until his death in 1945. FDR, as he is known, contracted the virus as an adult. He went to great lengths to hide his paralysis, fearing that public knowledge of his disability would end his political career.

FDR used leg braces and a cane as well as wheelchairs designed to look like nonmoving chairs. He and his staff pressured photographers to refrain from taking images of him in the chairs, so only a handful exist.

Currently, many disabled people serve as high-profile public servants, including Senator Tammy Duckworth (D-IL), who uses a wheelchair and prosthetic legs due to a war injury, and Carla Qualtrough, who serves as a Canadian member of parliament and the minister of employment, workforce development, and disability inclusion and is blind.

As Heumann later wrote in her memoir, *Being Heumann*, the advice her parents received was commonplace. "Kids with disabilities were considered a hardship, economically and socially." Erasing them could also save the family public shame. "People thought that when someone in your family had a disability it was because someone had done something wrong."

Heumann's parents didn't send her away. The Jewish immigrants had lost their families to the Nazis. They were determined to do whatever they could for their bright and lively daughter.

But when they tried to enroll Heumann in the local school, the school refused. In fact, no New York City school offered to enroll Heumann. At the time, few schools had ramps. Few buses had lifts for wheelchairs. Heumann couldn't even cross her own street easily because of high curbs. Although the school sent a teacher to her home, it was for less than three hours per week. At the time, it was not illegal to discriminate against people with disabilities.

Heumann's mother refused to give up. Eventually, when Heumann was nine years old, she attended a segregated class for disabled children in the basement of a school for the nondisabled. In 1961 Heumann enrolled in a public high school near her home, the first time she was in class with nondisabled children.

Heumann organized other students to protest the lack of access to most classrooms. "We were learning that despite what society might be telling us, we all had the same right as the non-disabled to contribute to our communities," Heumann later wrote. It was a lesson she learned well.

As important to Heumann were the summer camps she started attending, in particular Camp Jened. Launched in 1952 by families of children with cerebral palsy and run by self-described "hippies," Camp Jened was a revelation for Heumann. For the first time, she was away from her parents and able to engage with other kids without always being left behind because of her wheelchair. Like nondisabled teens, along with crafts and outdoor activities, they could smoke and have make-out sessions when counselors weren't looking.

Always social, she began to feel more her true self, she later realized. In 2020 the documentary *Crip Camp*, featuring found footage of one summer at Camp Jened, was nominated for an Academy Award. Amid the glitz of Hollywood, the documentary captured a joy that radiates through Heumann's frequent appearances. "The freedom we felt at camp was not just from our parents and our need for their daily assistance in order to live our lives," she wrote about the experience. "We were drunk on the freedom of not feeling like a burden, a feeling that was a constant companion in our lives outside of camp."

Heumann finished college, planning to become a teacher. But when she took the required physical, the Board of Education of the City of New York cited the paralysis of her legs as an excuse for discriminating against her and denying her a teaching license. "I wasn't contagious, but somehow I'd been deemed a contaminant."

Heumann tried to get the American Civil Liberties Union (ACLU) to support a lawsuit in 1969. But lawyers refused to meet with her, claiming that the denial of her teaching license was not discriminatory. (The

ACLU sent Heumann a formal apology for this response in 2021.) The organization's reasoning was that disabilities weren't explicitly included under the 1964 Civil Rights Act, which protects the right of Black people to vote. The ACLU wouldn't even allow her to come to the office to plead her case. Heumann realized that she—along with Vietnam veterans returning home without legs or arms, those born with disabilities, and those who had become disabled as they aged—were going to have to make themselves impossible to ignore.

Heumann talked to journalists and found a lawyer, who successfully sued New York City's Board of Education. In the fall of 1970 she began teaching in the same elementary school where she'd been a student. "We were learning from the Civil Rights Movement and from the Women's Rights Movement. We were learning from them about their activism and their ability to come together, not only to discuss problems but to discuss solutions. And what was born is what we call today the Disability Rights Movement."

Heumann soon transitioned from teaching to full-time activism with a new group called Disabled in Action. She focused on a federal bill called the Rehabilitation Act. In those dense paragraphs, she spotted Section 504. Specifically, the language would ban discrimination based on disability by anyone receiving federal funding.

"My mind churned, processing," she remembered. This was the first time the government acknowledged Americans with disabilities faced alarming discrimination. In essence, she realized, Section 504 was a kind of Civil Rights Act for the disabled.

DISABILITY AND DIVERSITY

One result of the disability rights movement is that people connect through disabilities. Diversity, Heumann notes, is not just around race, religion, and sexual orientation. Disabled people have visible and invisible disabilities and are from all racial, ethnic, and religious backgrounds and sexual orientations.

In an interview with Trevor Noah, host of the *The Daily Show*, Heumann pointed out that most people will become disabled in their lifetime, whether temporarily or permanently. Medical advances may address some disabilities. These advances can also mean that some who might have died due to injury, among them soldiers, can survive with permanent disability.

Access for the disabled helps everyone, including parents with children in strollers who use accessible ramps and elevators, Heumann told Noah. "I want people to stop feeling threatened by this reality and understand that this is a community that anyone can join during their lives. And everyone in the disabled community should be guaranteed their human rights."

Then president Richard M. Nixon vetoed the bill in 1972, prompting Heumann and 50 allies in Disabled in Action to mount their first-ever street protest, crowding wheelchairs and crutches onto streets near the Nixon campaign headquarters in Manhattan. Briefly, they managed to shut down traffic in one of the busiest areas of New York City. "Although we got no press coverage, we did get reported on in the evening traffic report," she remembered.

Heumann came to the attention of another activist, Ed Roberts, the first openly disabled student to enroll at the University of California, Berkeley, and the director of the Center for Independent Living, which promotes the rights of disabled people and helps them live independently. Roberts told Heumann that Berkeley wanted to recruit disabled students. He counseled her to apply for a master's degree and invited her to join the center's board of directors.

At first, the idea of leaving New York and her family terrified her. But Heumann eventually boarded a plane for California. For the first time, she lived independently. "I hired someone to come in the morning and the evening to help," she remembered. "As a result, I got to decide when I wanted to get up, when and what I wanted to eat, and when I wanted to go to sleep. I could go out on Saturday nights without worrying about how I'd get to bed!"

After completing her degree, Heumann moved to Washington, DC, to work for Senator Harrison Williams (D-NJ), known for his support for disability rights. By then, President Nixon had signed the Rehabilitation Act into law. However, his administration—and the one that followed, after he resigned in 1973 due to the Watergate scandal—did nothing to implement Section 504 and end legal discrimination.

Along with other disabled activists, Heumann worried that the delay would lead to the law being weakened. She and hundreds of others decided to occupy federal buildings across the country to protest.

By now back in the Bay Area, Heumann and other activists organized a protest in San Francisco. Before leaving her home on April 5, 1977, she packed one pair of extra underwear just in case.

After a round of fiery speeches, Heumann rallied hundreds of disabled and nondisabled people to storm the city's federal building. "The area teemed," she later wrote. "People were pushing chairs, leaning on crutches, holding white canes."

SECTION 504 PROTEST

Across the country, protesters refused to leave federal buildings in San Francisco; Denver; Washington, DC; and Los Angeles. This was a sit-in, a technique pioneered by the civil rights activists who inspired Heumann.

A sit-in is the act of protesters occupying an important site, refusing to leave until their demands are met. For disabled people, this meant facing hardships not immediately apparent to the nondisabled. Many protesters depended on personal assistants to use the bathroom or dress. Others needed regular medications.

Yet 150 people with disabilities stayed with Heumann, along with some personal assistants. For Heumann, such actions help make people who would otherwise be "invisible" more visible. The occupation continued until after officials signed the 504 regulations without changes.

As it turned out, Heumann underpacked. For the next 24 days, she and more than 100 others occupied the building, the spark for a national and international disability rights movement. In other cities, the occupiers left after the government cut off access to food, water, and telephones. But Heumann and the other San Francisco occupiers worked with the Black Panthers to bring in food. They used sign language to communicate with supporters outside. They even hosted a hearing led by the city's two congressional representatives.

Suddenly, the media interviewed people many had considered incapable of having an opinion. "We were seen as helpless and childlike, as the kind of people for whom you felt pity and raised money to cure their disease. Not the kind of people who fought back," she said.

Still, President Jimmy Carter refused to sign Section 504. So Heumann started a hunger strike, forgoing food until their demands were met. After almost a month, Heumann and her fellow protesters heard the news that the White House signed Section 504. They'd won their Civil Rights Act. And they'd just successfully concluded the longest sit-in protest in US history at the time.

Heumann went on to help pass the Americans with Disabilities Act (ADA), signed into law by President George H. W. Bush in 1990. She and others call the ADA "our Emancipation Proclamation act," since few modern laws have had a bigger impact on Americans' lives. In practice, the ADA makes it illegal for anyone or any organization that receives money from the federal government to discriminate against someone with a disability. New public buildings must have ramps. Curbs must be adjusted for wheelchairs. (Unfortunately, the ADA didn't require existing buildings to be retrofitted, so many remain inaccessible.) Sign language and accessible software is increasingly common.

In 2006 Heumann celebrated an international victory, the passage of the United Nations' Convention on the Rights of Persons with Disabilities, the first international human rights treaty to be adopted after the end of the Cold War. Heumann went on to work on disability issues for both the Bill Clinton and Barack Obama presidential administrations, as well as for the World Bank, an institution aimed at funding lower-income countries.

Perhaps more than many, Heumann knows that progress isn't permanent. Rights are fragile. She believes people must remain vigilant to fight against efforts to erase or limit the rights of others. President Donald J. Trump attempted to dismantle the Affordable Care Act, which provides many, including people with disabilities, with health care. His White House also took down the pages that are usable by accessibility software on its public website. Trump famously mocked a disabled reporter in a campaign speech. "Human rights are like salamanders," Heumann wrote in her memoir. "You don't notice they're disappearing until suddenly you realize they've gone."

But Heumann and the disability rights movement aren't going anywhere. Her takeaway? "My story isn't really my story. It's our story," she told Trevor Noah on *The Daily Show*. "We believed that every single person had a role in producing the change. We knew our success would hinge on collaboration. Our power would only come from the people who identified with, and felt ownership of, a movement."

DISCUSSION QUESTIONS

1. Think of some everyday activities you do without thinking. What are the steps you would take to accomplish the same activities if you had lost an ability you need to do these things? How would this change your life?

2. What branch of government must create regulations (not laws)? Which branch enforces them? Do you think Heumann's activist strategy was more successful than a legal strategy might have been?

3. Heumann says that progress isn't necessarily permanent. What are the ways that you've seen that progress can sometimes start and then stop?

HUMANS ARE ANIMALS ARE HUMANS: INGRID NEWKIRK

🏳 **ANIMAL RIGHTS**

👤 **1949–**

📍 **UNITED KINGDOM**

It doesn't matter who the victim is.
It's that they're victimized.

As a young woman, Ingrid Newkirk's favorite food was liver. When she ate steak, she liked it raw. But the day her neighbor moved away, Newkirk started a journey that pitted her taste for meat against her love of animals.

The animals won. As the president and founder of People for the Ethical Treatment of Animals (PETA), Newkirk is one of the most influential and controversial rights activists of the 20th century.

She often tells the story of how she came to be a passionate animal rights advocate. In her 20s, she was living in Virginia. A next-door neighbor announced that she was leaving and would abandon some cats. Newkirk gathered them up and drove them to the nearest animal shelter. As she later told a journalist, "When I arrived at the shelter, the woman said, 'I'll take them into the back, and we will just put them down there.'"

Born in the United Kingdom and raised in India before moving to America, Newkirk thought *put down* meant to put them in a room. With horror, she later learned that the woman had killed the cats without even examining them.

Newkirk had been studying to be a stockbroker. Instead, she changed course and took a kennel-cleaner job at that same shelter. Every day, she witnessed animals being killed in cruel ways and grew determined to ensure that their last experience on earth was painless. She also saw how some people abused animals. "Driving home every night, I would cry just thinking about it. And I just felt, to my bones, this cannot be right," she told the *New Yorker* in 2003.

An only child, she'd had a beloved dog, Sean, who slept in her bed. Her mother, too, taught her about compassion. "My mother used to say, 'It doesn't matter who suffers. It's that they suffer and what you can do to help them.'"

Newkirk took a job as a deputy sheriff in Montgomery County, Maryland, then took charge of animal disease control for the District of Columbia Commission on Public Health. She became convinced that there was no distinction between mistreating a dog or cat and mistreating any other animal. It wasn't enough to feel sorry for them. She felt compelled to do something.

With colleague Alex Pacheco, whom she met at the animal shelter, she founded PETA in 1980. PETA's motto is "Animals are not ours to experiment on, eat, wear, or use for entertainment, or abuse in any other way." The group started with a handful of volunteers. Like her, they believed that the defense of animals needed to be forceful.

In the summer of 1981, Newkirk and Pacheco planned to get inside a nearby federally funded laboratory that was using animals for research. The laboratory had 16 crab-eating macaques and one rhesus monkey. A psychologist would damage their brains, then shock the monkeys into using their paralyzed limbs. The purpose was to see if the monkeys' brains would remap and allow them to use their limbs. That information, researchers believed, might help human stroke victims regain the use of their arms and legs.

HOBBIES

One of Newkirk's hobbies is following Formula 1 racing. Her first husband was a professional driver. She's also a fan of Japanese sumo wrestling.

But Pacheco discovered a kind of monkey torture chamber. The animals were kept in tiny, rusted cages. No veterinarian tended their open wounds. With no feeding dishes, dry food fell into the trays below the cages that contained feces, so the monkeys had to pick through their own waste for food. In their efforts to escape, some monkeys tore off fingers on the wire of their cages.

A trained law enforcement officer, Newkirk helped gather evidence, including photographs. After consulting with experts, she and Pacheco took their case to the police. Now known as the Silver Spring monkeys case, this led to the nation's first arrest and criminal conviction of a scientist for cruelty to animals. The case also helped convince the US

Congress to toughen the Animal Welfare Act, which requires that minimum standards of care and treatment be provided for certain animals bred for commercial sale, used in research, transported commercially, or exhibited to the public.

Like Eglantyne Jebb (from the chapter "The White Flame"), the founder of Save the Children, Newkirk discovered that she had a talent for publicity. "We would be worthless if we were just polite and didn't make any waves," she told the *New Yorker*.

PETA followed on its success in the Silver Spring monkeys case with other, high-profile actions. To some, these were stunts, but others praised the group's initiative. PETA forced the closure of a huge horse slaughterhouse in Texas. Another effort repeated its focus on animal research. The group obtained videotapes taken at the University of Pennsylvania Head Injury Clinic that showed pistons crushing the skulls of baboons. Those experiments ended after PETA staged a four-day sit-in at the National Institutes of Health.

There were other protests as well. In 1996, a PETA member threw a dead raccoon onto the plate of fashion magazine editor Anna Wintour, who often wore fur. She reportedly coolly told the waiter to take it away.

Every year since 2002, PETA has staged a Running of the Nudes in Pamplona, Spain, at the same time as the famed Running of the Bulls. The event with bulls started as a religious festival but now draws thousands of locals and tourists to the town's narrow streets to run in front of a small herd of terrified bulls. PETA's counterrun involves humans running naked save for a set of plastic horns or a red scarf. Newkirk argues

that the bulls are stressed by the unfamiliar noises and crowds and sometimes stumble into walls, fall, and injure themselves or even get killed.

The event also celebrates bullfighting, a Spanish and Latin American
tradition involving a matador, or bullfighter, ritually and slowly killing a
bull in front of thousands of spectators. PETA has accused the sponsors
of bullfights of drugging the animals, feeding them debilitating laxatives,
shaving their horns to keep them off balance, and rubbing petroleum
jelly into their eyes to impair their vision.

Newkirk is controversial. Unlike most rights activists, Newkirk doesn't
distinguish between humans and animals. "When it comes to feelings like
hunger, pain, and thirst, a rat is a pig is a dog is a boy," she says.

A vegan, Newkirk neither uses, eats, nor wears anything from an
animal. Even honey is off-limits, since its production depends on smok-
ing out a hive and taking the food bees have made to sustain themselves.

She believes this is something young people especially understand.
"When I grew up, some 72 years ago, we had ivory ornaments on the man-
telpiece and meat for every meal, every circus was full of wild animals, girls
like me aspired to own a fur coat (and I did at 19)," she says. "Today, children grow up hearing about animal rights and seeing exposés of factory
farming and the exotic skins trade, and they have options that they love,
including alternatives to stealing feathers, skin, wool, and fur from animals
who were born with them and need them as their own coats. . . . It's a new
world, and each generation is more aware than the last."

In 2014 Newkirk published a will that both was legal and represented
her deeply held views. Even in death, Newkirk wants people to think

about how we treat animals. She requested that the "meat of her body, or a portion thereof, be used for a human barbecue, to remind the world that the meat of a corpse is all flesh, regardless of whether it comes from a human being or another animal and that flesh foods are not needed; and that her skin be removed and made into leather products, such as purses, to remind the world that human skin and the skin of other animals is the same and that neither is 'fabric' or needed."

LEONARDO DA VINCI

Newkirk often talks about Renaissance artist Leonardo da Vinci. Born in 1452 in Italy's Tuscany region, Da Vinci was a painter, engineer, scientist, astronomer, anatomist, botanist, sculptor, and architect. Among his most famous works are *The Last Supper*, a fresco in the convent of Santa Maria delle Grazie in Milan, and the *Mona Lisa*, in the Louvre Museum in Paris, France.

Da Vinci was also a lifelong vegetarian. He once wrote, "The day will come when men such as I will look upon the murder of animals the way they now look upon the murder of men."

PETA largely succeeded in its campaign against animal fur with the I'd Rather Go Naked Than Wear Fur campaign in the 1990s. Other campaigns against the use of animals in circuses and Sea World–style animal shows have also been successful. In 2017 Ringling Bros. and Barnum & Bailey Circus closed. Belgium, Greece, Malta, and Italy ban circus animals entirely.

HUMAN AND ANIMAL RIGHTS

Newkirk sees a clear connection between rights for humans and for animals. For her, all living beings deserve to live free from "needless pain and unnecessary suffering; . . . being unfairly imprisoned; kept in involuntary servitude; treated with disrespect, for one's inherent interests; or harmed out of spite, [out of] convenience, or just because someone has the power to do so."

The race, religion, species, nationality, gender, physical ability, or mental acuity doesn't matter. "All that counts is whether they are being treated appropriately, fairly, and with respect."

PETA opposes the use of animal tests for any reason and has helped develop artificial lungs and other sophisticated methods of testing that don't depend on animals. The group also opposes testing household products and cosmetics on animals, prompting brands like Dove, Secret, and Herbal Essences to adopt official bans on these methods. Many contemporary brands now proudly advertise how their products are developed without animal testing and display PETA's Global Beauty without Bunnies logo on their products and websites.

Clothing companies like H&M and Gap have agreed to PETA's appeals to not carry exotic skins, to avoid angora and mohair, and to cut ties with an alpaca supplier. Many more are making the switch to vegan clothing lines. PETA and other animal rights groups have also succeeded in convincing fast-food restaurants like Burger King and Wendy's to offer vegan options. Restaurants and grocery stores now offer a variety of vegan products.

Newkirk knows that her often dramatic approach doesn't please everyone, including some animal rights groups. Newkirk sees herself in the tradition of anti–slave trade campaigners. When slavery was legal, many accepted it as normal.

"In my 20s, I was deeply inspired by Sojourner Truth," she told a journalist. Truth was born into slavery in New York; after she gained her freedom, she was targeted by proslavery activists who set fire to Truth's boarding house and threw stones at her. Newkirk describes Truth as a "slight Black woman, [who] would elbow her way into a crowd, stand on a box, and ask them to examine their prejudices toward women and enslaved Blacks."

For Newkirk, Truth's actions inspire her to push the envelope and demand radical change. "If you say something someone already agrees with," she notes, "then what's the point?"

DISCUSSION QUESTIONS

1. In your opinion, which animals are pets and why? What obligations do humans have to pets that they don't have to other animals? Is scientific testing on animals other than pets necessary to keep humans safe?

2. The Silver Springs monkeys experiment helped scientists develop therapies for adults who suffered traumatic brain

injuries. Through what's called constraint-induced movement therapy, some patients can regain the use of partially paralyzed limbs. Does that fact change your opinion about using animals in medical experiments?

3. Do you agree with Newkirk that animals have emotions? How do you tell? Does an animal have self-control or free will? Should animals have the same rights as human beings?

RECLAIMING THE MEANING OF PEACE: JODY WILLIAMS

⚑ **THE CAMPAIGN TO END LAND MINES**

👤 **1950–**

📍 **UNITED STATES**

There's nothing magical about bringing about change—it's about converting your concern into action.

Advances in weapon technologies reshape the world. They can also lead to horrific loss of life.

In the Middle Ages, the English longbow ranked among the most feared weapons of war. Roughly the height of a human being, the bow could launch fatal arrows three times as fast as shorter bows and was called "the machine gun of the medieval era." Arrows shot from longbows could pierce even metal armor.

In Europe, the longbow's dominance ended with the introduction of the cannon, a technology first developed in China. Hurtling balls of iron packed with gunpowder could decimate a line of bowmen and demolish castle walls and fortifications. With the invention of airplanes, armies could not only see farther but also cross oceans, as the Japanese did in the attack on the US naval base at Pearl Harbor in 1941.

Four years after Pearl Harbor, the US introduced a new weapon: the nuclear bomb. On August 6, 1945, an American bomber dropped a 10,000-pound nuclear bomb on the city of Hiroshima. Three days later, the Americans dropped a second, more powerful bomb on Nagasaki, 260 miles to the southwest of Hiroshima. Combined, 120,000 people died instantly. Over the next weeks, hundreds of thousands more perished from radiation sickness. Unlike the longbow and the cannon, which can be targeted at soldiers, the nuclear bomb is a weapon of mass destruction and causes overwhelmingly civilian casualties.

THE NUCLEAR BOMB

Both Hiroshima and Nagasaki manufactured military supplies, but the US didn't choose them for their importance to Japan's war effort. The Americans intended for the nuclear bombs to cause massive civilian casualties and compel the Japanese to surrender.

The Soviets were the next country to detonate a nuclear bomb in August 1949, in a test. Currently, nine countries have nuclear weapons: Russia, the United States, France, China, the United Kingdom, Pakistan, India, Israel, and North Korea.

Jody Williams was born five years after the bombs, nicknamed "Little Boy" and "Fat Man," detonated. But she remembers clearly how the fear of nuclear attack permeated her small Vermont town. Like other students, she had to practice hiding under her desk, making her feel "anything but safe."

So did a much more present threat—the neighborhood kids who bullied her older brother, Steve. He'd been born deaf. "They liked hearing his sounds of fear and just laughed because it was so strange sounding," she told one journalist.

The injustice enraged her. Williams's blue eyes are large and expressive, and she smiles frequently. She has a brash, direct way of speaking, as if she has no time to waste. Leaping to her brother's defense became a lifelong determination to stand up for others. "Once you defend somebody and cause a bully to stop bullying, you realize what I do and say matters. That grew into the larger philosophical question: do you sit back and do nothing in a world that is so unequal and so unfair? Or do you do something? I ultimately found the path to doing something."

Williams graduated from college, married, and divorced. Yet she didn't feel her life had a purpose. A move to Washington, DC, brought her in touch with activists who opposed the US war in El Salvador. As she learned more, she felt a familiar outrage. Bullies had persecuted her brother. In college, she'd protested the Vietnam War, believing that one powerful country, the United States, was bullying a weaker one. How could the US promote democracy while at the same time support the abusive Salvadoran military?

Simple outrage, she knew, accomplished nothing. "The only thing that might help would be to do something to make it different."

She threw herself into organizing protests. After completing a master's degree in international studies, she switched to providing medical aid to needy Central Americans. The work was often dangerous. A self-described member of a Salvadoran death squad, infamous for killing leftists and human rights activists, raped Williams in her hotel room. She only spoke about this publicly years later, in a 2006 performance of playwright Eve Ensler's *Vagina Monologues*.

"I felt it was time to use the example to tell women they didn't have to let horrible experiences ruin their lives. I didn't let it ruin mine," she wrote in her memoir, *My Name Is Jody Williams*.

Williams decided to take a break and get what she called a "regular nine-to-five job" in 1991. Then a friend of a friend asked her to help organize a coalition of groups to press for a ban on land mines. Since the end of World War II, the use of these mines had spread throughout the world. Each year, tens of thousands of civilians were killed or maimed.

Williams remembered the nuclear bomb drills she'd done as kid. Land mines seemed less dangerous than an explosive that could wipe out a large city. She asked herself, *Why dedicate my time to abolishing land mines?*

Her answer changed over the course of her life. Whereas nuclear weapons are highly sophisticated and expensive to develop and maintain, land mines are simple and cheap to manufacture. When the land mine campaign started in 1992, so many locations had been mined that an average of 26,000 civilians—a fifth of them children—died or lost limbs each year. Over 100 million mines threatened anyone who stepped on them.

Unlike a bullet fired by a solider, a land mine can't be aimed, meaning it can't distinguish between a civilian and combatant. In poor countries especially, no one paid for land mines to be removed after a war ended, meaning that they continued to maim and kill.

Land mines cause devastating injuries, including blindness, hearing loss, and the loss of limbs. By the 1990s, land mines killed civilians in Cambodia, Libya, Bosnia, Mozambique, and dozens more countries. Meanwhile, no nuclear bomb has been detonated as a part of hostilities since 1945.

"It wasn't about changing our world from a planet of war into one of peace overnight," Williams realized. "It was about banning one weapon, which started a process of change."

From her work in Central America, Williams knew a lot about activism but little about land mines. She dug into research. She was also relentless, talking on the phone, sending documents, and planning strategy. For many months, she was the campaign's lone employee. Her main job was to glue the far-flung group together in a time before the Internet.

Williams would never call herself shy or soft-spoken. Some people, Williams told a reporter, "have got a problem with my personality. I don't care."

At one United Nations conference, she cheered as campaigners built a fake minefield at the door so diplomats would trigger explosive sounds as they left their meeting to refill on coffee or use the bathroom. "It had grass and shrubs and sensors underneath," she remembers. The purpose was to give them a sense of urgency. "When someone stepped on the sensor it would make a bang as if it were a landmine."

NOBEL WOMEN'S INITIATIVE

Along with Shirin Ebadi (from the chapter "The Tightrope Walker") and Williams, the other cofounders of the Nobel Women's Initiative included Rigoberta Menchú Tum (Guatemala) and Betty Williams and Mairead Maguire (Northern Ireland). Wangari Maathai of Kenya belonged until her death in 2011. Today, the initiative includes Leymah Gbowee (Liberia) and Tawakkol Karman (Yemen).

One early supporter was US Senator Patrick J. Leahy (D-VT), later joined by Canada's minister of foreign affairs, Lloyd Axworthy. But the most powerful voices were those of land mine survivors. Tun Channareth, known as Reth, a former soldier, lost both legs to a land mine in his native Cambodia. At the time, there were over 10 million land mines in the country. In despair after his injury, Reth tried to kill himself. Then he found new purpose in helping others, including by making wheelchairs. In pressing for the treaty, he says he "begged them to stop mining and stop making mines, stop producing mines. Please help us."

In only a few years, the International Campaign to Ban Landmines had 1,300 member organizations in 95 countries. Partners included governments as well as the International Committee of the Red Cross, which determined that land mines were indiscriminate weapons and therefore violated the laws of war.

In 1997 the campaign achieved a huge victory. After complex negotiations, the United Nations and 122 member states adopted the Mine Ban Treaty. The treaty bans the use, production, stockpiling, and transfer of land mines. The treaty also requires countries to destroy their existing land mines, clear mined areas, and assist survivors of land mines. As of 2021, 164 states in all have signed the treaty. One country that has yet to sign is the United States.

THE UNITED STATES AND LAND MINES

The US has banned the production, acquisition, and transfer of land mines except in the Korean Peninsula, where the US helps maintain a militarized border between North and South Korea. Currently, South Korea—which did not sign the Mine Ban Treaty—continues to produce land mines and maintains a stockpile believed to contain anywhere from 500,000 to 2 million mines. The demilitarized zone separating North and South Korea is among the most heavily mined areas in the world.

That same year, 1997, Williams and the campaign were awarded the Nobel Peace Prize. Though some governments also contributed substantially to the treaty, the prize committee chose to highlight workers like Williams. That decision, Williams said, makes it "very clear that ordinary people can and do have important parts to play in contributing to peace."

While Williams celebrated the recognition, she also worried that people could draw the wrong lesson. "The 'change happens overnight' part can be very disempowering to people. . . . You have to help people understand that everybody adds a little element, and then things change. It can seem sudden, but there's nothing sudden about it. The process flows, and then you reach your goal. But it takes time. And reaching the goal might not even happen in your lifetime."

With fellow Nobel Prize laureate Shirin Ebadi, Williams founded the Nobel Women's Initiative to support and amplify the efforts of women around the world working for peace, justice, and equality. Returning to one of her earliest issues, Williams launched a new campaign in the city of Hiroshima in 2010 to ban all nuclear weapons. Williams called on countries to stop the further development of nuclear weapons and ban those weapons outright.

"In my view, what we need today is people getting up and taking action to reclaim the meaning of peace," Williams said later that year. "It's not a dirty word. It's hard work every single day. And if each of us who cares about the different things we care about got up off our butts and volunteered as much time as we could, we would change this world, we would save this world. And we can't wait for the other guy. We have to do it ourselves."

DISCUSSION QUESTIONS

1. During the Cold War, most people accepted the threat of nuclear attack and prepared for it. What are you trained to fear and protect yourself against today?

2. Jody Williams said, "It was about banning one weapon, which started a process of change." What one device or invention would you ban to end some human suffering?

3. Like Henri Dunant (from the chapter "The Man in White") and Benjamin Ferencz ("A Case for Humanity"), Williams's work is about limiting the devastation of war, not ending war outright. Yet all three became passionate antiwar activists. Is their gradual approach effective, or should activists spend more energy trying to ban war?

THE LONG ROAD:
S. JAMES ANAYA

⚑ INDIGENOUS RIGHTS

👤 1958–

📍 UNITED STATES

Modern human rights is the open door that Indigenous people walk through to gain recognition.

S. James Anaya didn't begin to explore his Indigenous identity until he was a law student. His heritage is Apache; Purépecha, from the highlands of Mexico's Michoacán state; and Mexican. Linguists still puzzle over the Purépecha language, as it isn't linked to languages spoken by other Indigenous groups.

Indigenous means the living descendants of distinct communities with ancestral roots in lands invaded by others, especially Europeans. Anaya's father was a US Marine and then a Baptist preacher, and his mother was a teacher. Anaya spent his childhood mostly away from where his parents grew up in the tiny town of Central, New Mexico, now part of Santa Clara. "I only thought about my Indigenous identity when I was discriminated against, when people would call me things," he remembers.

Like many from the American Southwest, Anaya has deep roots on both sides of the US-Mexico border as well as in Indigenous, Mexican, and White culture. He has a broad face with a boyish shock of black hair and a lively intensity in his eyes. Anaya also inherited a legacy that combines the violence of the extermination of Indigenous people with fierce histories of resistance and resurgence. "The history of European colonialism and empire building created scars that are still felt today," he says.

At Harvard Law School, his history inspired him to learn to use the law to help Indigenous people. One of the figures who inspired him was Deskaheh, the Haudenosaunee confederation chief who traveled to Geneva in 1923 to address the League of Nations, the short-lived precursor to the United Nations. To travel, Deskaheh carried a passport issued by his people, not the Canadian government.

Deskaheh thought he could use international diplomacy and the law to defend Indigenous people. Also known as the Iroquois, this confederation stretches east and north from Pennsylvania into modern-day Canada and includes the Mohawk, Oneida, Onondaga, Cayuga, and Seneca peoples.

Deskaheh argued that the Iroquois were equal to other nations and had the same rights. They refused to be forced to be part of Canada. Although Deskaheh failed to gain international support for Iroquois autonomy, his vision for Indigenous independence inspired Anaya. "Even though his efforts did not bear immediate fruit," Anaya said, "that same optimism was present in subsequent efforts by Indigenous peoples to appeal to the international community."

THE APACHE

The Apache are an Indigenous people from the American Southwest and northern Mexico. The Apache language is part of a group known as Athabascan, spoken as far north as modern-day Alaska.

When White settlers began taking Apache land in the 1800s, Cochise, a Chiricahua Apache, was among the Apache's greatest leaders. The Apache attempted to live alongside newcomers, but as more settlers arrived and began attacking them, Cochise and others tried to drive them away. But they were no match for well-armed, trained cavalry. In 1872 Cochise negotiated a surrender and moved to a reservation, where he died in 1874.

Other Apache refused to submit. Among the most famous is Goyahkla, better known as Geronimo. Goyahkla helped lead a years-long resistance and was among the last Native Americans to surrender, in 1886. Having spent over two decades as prisoners of war, he and his group moved from the Southwest to Florida then back to Fort Sill, Oklahoma. The US forcibly sent many Apache children to distant boarding schools, where they were beaten for speaking their native language or observing their customs.

The first such school was Carlisle Indian Industrial School in Carlisle, Pennsylvania, a model for the more than 450 boarding schools that later opened in the US. The school's unofficial motto, coined by its first director, was "Kill the Indian, and save the man." At Carlisle, dozens of Indigenous students died of tuberculosis and other diseases while away from their families.

Goyahkla died in Oklahoma in 1909. His last words were reported to be, "I should have never surrendered. I should have fought until I was the last man alive."

One of Anaya's first cases as a lawyer was to help restore land rights to a Pueblo community. Located in the American southwest, the Pueblo are among the oldest cultures in North America and comprise over 20 individual groups, including Acoma, Zuni, and Hopi. "This felt good, helping the tribe to be in control of their lands and their own development," he explained.

In another case, Anaya helped sue the *Albuquerque Journal* newspaper for sending a news helicopter over a Pueblo feast day ceremony to take photographs. Feast days are deeply spiritual. Taking pictures is not permitted. For Anaya, more than any punishment, the lawsuit helped promote greater awareness of Indigenous autonomy and vibrant culture. "Unless the broader society is sensitized about the concerns of Indigenous peoples and accepts the legitimacy of their recognized rights, it will always be difficult to sustain the enjoyment of those rights."

Anaya took a position as a law professor to advance knowledge about Indigenous peoples and the issues they face. In the 1970s and 1980s, he joined a group of human rights and Indigenous activists who wanted to use human rights not only to defend rights but also to protect claims on ancestral lands and culture. Anaya believes that Indigenous peoples have both individual human rights and collective rights to self-determination and land as a matter of international law. "For Indigenous people, land represents the people in a very fundamental sense."

An opportunity to defend land rights arose with the Miskito community in Nicaragua. Settled along the Atlantic coast of Honduras and Nicaragua, the Miskito are Indigenous mixed with European, African, and Asian immigrants. In the 1980s a brutal civil war enveloped the region. This was the same war that concerned Juan Méndez (from the chapter "Determination, Patience, Insistence") as the director of Americas Watch.

In Nicaragua, the rebel group called the Sandinista National Liberation Front, or Sandinistas, won. But many Miskito rejected the Sandinista belief that Indigenous identity was a relic to be swept away in the interests of building working-class solidarity. Believing that they would be wiped out, some Miskito allied with US-backed counterrebels, the contras. The Sandinistas retaliated by attempting to force Miskito to flee their land.

In 1996 Anaya helped broker a peace agreement that included the Nicaraguan government's recognition of Indigenous rights. But that didn't fully resolve the question of rights for the Indigenous peoples in the country. A year earlier, the Mayagna community of Awas Tingni, also on Nicaragua's east coast, filed a lawsuit to block the government from allowing a foreign company to log their ancestral land. The Mayagna see themselves as the protectors of some of the last surviving primary rainforest in Central America, an area of high biodiversity.

THE SANDINISTAS

The Sandinista National Liberation Front (Frente Sandinista de Liberación Nacional) named itself for a hero of the Nicaraguan resistance to US military occupation from 1927 to 1933, César Augusto Sandino. The organizers were also inspired by the Cuban Revolution.

Sandinistas believed they could unite Nicaraguan workers and peasants against US-backed elites. But not until late in their development did the Sandinistas acknowledge that some Nicaraguans don't consider themselves mestizo, or mixed, between Spanish, Black, and Indigenous, but rather maintain an Indigenous identity.

Although the Nicaraguan Constitution recognizes the right of Indigenous communities to their lands, the government did little to protect those rights. When that lawsuit failed, Anaya and the Awas Tingni presented a petition before the Inter-American Commission on Human Rights. The commission brings cases before the Inter-American Court of Human Rights, which resolves legal disputes involving countries that are members of the Organization of American States. This is the same court that helped define "disappearances" as crimes against humanity that countries must prosecute (discussed in the chapter "Determination, Patience, Insistence").

The case was the first Indigenous land dispute to be addressed by this court. In 2001 the court decided in favor of the Awas Tingni, the first time in history Indigenous land rights had been upheld as a matter of international law. In its ruling, the court declared that "for Indigenous communities the relationship with the land is not merely a question of possession and production, but it is also a material and spiritual element which they should fully enjoy, as well as a means to preserve their cultural heritage and pass it onto future generations."

THE INTER-AMERICAN COURT OF HUMAN RIGHTS

The Inter-American Court of Human Rights (IACHR) is an independent body of the Organization of American States, an association of Western Hemisphere countries, like a regional United Nations.

The IACHR doesn't issue criminal verdicts but can mount investigations into member countries and compel those found guilty of human rights violations to pay financial reparations, and change or adopt laws. The IACHR also follows up with regular reports to check if countries are obeying its decisions.

The court ordered the government to recognize Awas Tingni lands and establish legal mechanisms to do the same with other Indigenous communities in Nicaragua. But for Indigenous people around the world, the decision was a landmark, recognizing some of what Deskaheh had argued before the League of Nations, that Indigenous people should have a say over their homes. In the words of Armstrong Wiggins, a Miskito activist, "This ruling requires every country in the Americas to rethink the way it deals with the Indigenous peoples within its borders."

Anaya points out that the people of Awas Tingni didn't set out to create an international legal precedent. Yet that's what they did, compelling governments under international pressure and law.

Anaya also worked for a new international declaration on behalf of Indigenous rights. Passed at the United Nations in 2007 by a majority of 143 states in favor, the Declaration on the Rights of Indigenous Peoples establishes a universal framework for the survival, dignity, and well-being of Indigenous peoples. For Anaya, colonization and powerlessness for Indigenous peoples are gradually becoming part of the past as communities gain control over their own lands and futures. "What's required is new thinking about new models, new partnerships," Anaya says. "Unbridled state control of resources on Indigenous lands is a thing of the past."

In 2008 Anaya began work as the UN special rapporteur on the rights of Indigenous peoples, traveling the world to advocate for their rights. His advocacy came at an especially important moment. Around the world, Indigenous peoples are on the front lines of climate change, after a history of being targeted for removal and exploitation. In areas like Nicaragua's Pacific coast, water levels are rising. On Navajo lands in the American Southwest, severe drought has reduced the availability of drinking and irrigation water.

Yet Anaya believes that solutions are possible if people work together. Speaking of Chief Deskaheh, he says, "Even though his efforts did not bear immediate fruit, that same optimism was present in subsequent efforts by Indigenous peoples to appeal to the international community. That same optimism allowed Indigenous peoples, once having gained a foothold in the UN, to propose and imagine a day when there would be a Declaration on the Rights of Indigenous Peoples. And that same optimism now helps drive the multiple efforts across the globe in multiple settings to see the rights enshrined in the Declaration made reality in Indigenous peoples' everyday lives."

DISCUSSION QUESTIONS

1. Can you think of rituals or places where it is not OK to take a picture? Should you ask before taking photos of places that you are invited to?

2. Do you think that governments should be able to sell the natural resources where Indigenous people are still living, even if the colonization took place generations (or centuries) ago? Is there a difference between lands from which a people were forcibly removed and have now returned and lands where Indigenous people never left?

3. What are meaningful ways to both acknowledge the wrongs done to Indigenous peoples and recognize and celebrate the vibrant communities that continue to be a part of many nations?

THE REPORTER:
ANNA POLITKOVSKAYA

⚑ **FREEDOM OF THE PRESS**
👤 **1958-2006**
📍 **RUSSIA**

My job is very simple as I see it.
I report everything I see.

Anna Politkovskaya could have left Russia for safety at any moment. Her family, terrified for her, urged her to leave. But Politkovskaya refused.

In 2002 she told a British journalist why. A passionate believer in press freedom and the rights of Russians to know what their government is doing, she believed leaving Russia was a betrayal. "The only thing to do is to take this to the bitter end, so that no one can say that when things became difficult, I ran away."

The daughter of Ukrainian diplomats, Politkovskaya was born in New York and was an American citizen. She had sharp features and a pixie haircut. She spoke with a restless, nervous energy. Her commitment to reporting didn't mean she didn't enjoy life. In her Moscow apartment, she kept an African gray parrot named Vakha, a common name in Chechnya, a Russian province where she did much of her reporting.

146

After graduating from Moscow University, her options were limited. At the time, the Soviet Union jailed reporters who wrote critical stories. Some published what are known as *samizdat*, secret pamphlets and flyers. But the Soviet secret police, then called the KGB, had informants everywhere. Writers and other dissidents could be sent to prison for long sentences or even vanish.

THE COLD WAR

The Bolshevik Revolution of 1917 brought Communists to power in the former Russian empire. They created the Soviet Union, which swallowed up much of Central and Eastern Europe and became a world power.

At the same time, the United States became the most powerful country in the world. For most of the 20th century, human rights were framed by what became known as the Cold War, the decades-long struggle for dominance between the US and the Soviet Union.

Each tended to overlook human rights abuses that occurred within their own borders or by their allies. Only in the 1970s did this begin to shift, as grassroots movements, nongovernmental organizations, and smaller countries promoted human rights separate from the interests of powerful countries.

Politkovskaya took a job with *Izvestiya*, which means "news" in Russian, the official publication of the Central Executive Committee of the Supreme Soviet. The only other legal paper was *Pravda*, or "truth," published by the equally official Communist Party. As Russians often joked, "There's no news in *Pravda* and no truth in *Izvestiya*."

She began writing for the state airline and enjoyed the perks of free tickets to explore the country. Russia is enormous, stretching from its eastern coast near Japan to the edge of Europe. Her travels coincided with a period of perestroika, or restructuring, the Soviet government's loosening of controls on politics, speech, and the economy in the mid-1980s.

At the same time, centuries-old resentments over what ethnic groups controlled what areas began to simmer. Businessmen hoping to make their fortunes began eyeing lucrative resources like oil and hydropower.

The Berlin Wall, which separated capitalist West Berlin from Communist East Berlin, fell in 1989. Suddenly, regions like Chechnya wanted independence. For centuries, Chechnya had sometimes worked with and sometimes battled the Russian empire. During the Bolshevik Revolution that led to the Soviet Union, Chechen fighters backed the Communists and were rewarded when Chechnya became an autonomous republic, one of several allowed to teach in its native language, Chechen.

That peace didn't last. Like the rest of the country, Chechnya endured repeated famine as well as violent waves of political repression. Joseph Stalin, the Soviet dictator from 1927 to 1953, deported millions of Chechens from their homes in 1944, believing wrongly that many had supported the invading German army. When the Chechens declared independence in 1991, few could say quite how a new government or economy would work.

But for Russia, independence was seen as a threat. Chechnya is oil-rich. If the Chechens became independent, so might other provinces. Russia would lose billions in income from taxes and fees.

Moscow rushed to block Chechen independence, then blockaded the province from receiving food and other basic supplies. In 1994, Russian troops poured into Chechnya. They met stiff opposition, including from former Soviet military officers who were Chechen and had switched sides.

Russian artillery pounded cities like Grozny, the Chechen capital. High-rises looked like a giant had ripped out large chunks, as if devouring a stone cake. Survivors saved what little they could in wheelbarrows, trundled over roads blasted by explosives.

For their part, some Chechens seemed almost eager to attack Russian civilians. In 1995 Chechen militants seized over a thousand hostages, mostly patients, nurses, and doctors, in a hospital in southern Russia. Hundreds died before negotiations led to the release of the survivors.

Poorly equipped and fed, the Russian military withdrew from Chechnya in 1996. But the Chechens couldn't form a government and began fighting among themselves. By the end of 1997 Chechnya was in chaos as warlords fought over control and money. Two years later, with Vladimir Putin as president, Russia unleashed a ferocious campaign meant to bring Chechnya back under Moscow's control.

That was when Politkovskaya began traveling to the war-torn province. She'd helped start a newspaper, *Novaya Gazeta* ("new newspaper"), a fiercely independent voice. With its Muslim majority, extensive oil reserves, history of opposing Russian rule, and brutal conflict, Chechnya seemed to crystallize the hopes and dangers of the moment. In 1999 Politkovskaya made the first of what would be dozens of reporting trips.

WOMEN AND WAR JOURNALISM

Many still believe that war reporting is mainly for men. But women have always provided essential news on wars.

For instance, American journalist Jane Cazneau reported on the Mexican-American conflict in 1846. Austrian writer Alice Schalek covered World War I for the German press. Clare Hollingworth, from Britain, wrote about witnessing German forces massing at the Polish border prior to the 1939 invasion. During the Vietnam War, French photographer Catherine Leroy became the first accredited journalist to parachute with the US Army's 173rd Airborne Brigade in Operation Junction City. In 2021 one of the most prominent journalists covering the victory of the Taliban in Afghanistan was CNN's Clarissa Ward.

Unlike other reporters who seemed eager to experience the thrill of war reporting, Politkovskaya said she was "afraid of everything that shoots." Yet she was determined to write from the point of view of those trapped in the violence. Her reporting was vivid, sometimes graphic. Even her own newspaper "cut out the toughest parts," she said, for fear of losing readers sickened by the suffering.

Some Russians blamed Politkovskaya and other reporters for inflaming tensions with their descriptions of torture, massacres, and rape.

"People call the newspaper and send letters with one and the same question," she once wrote. "Why are you writing about this? Why are you scaring us? Why do we need to know this? For one simple reason: as contemporaries of this war, we will be held responsible for it. The classic Soviet excuse of not being there and not taking part in anything personally won't work."

Her writing has a breathless quality that conveys a constant sense of urgency and threat. Always, she focused on human beings, be they terrified Russian soldiers, orphaned children, or starving grandmothers. She wrote in *A Small Corner of Hell: Dispatches from Chechnya*:

Here are the helicopters, going for another round. They fly so low that you can see the gunners' hands and faces. Some say that they can even see their eyes. But this is fear talking. The main thing is their legs, dangling carelessly in the open hatches. As if they didn't come to kill, but to let their tired feet get some fresh air. Their feet are big and scary, and the soles almost seem to touch our faces. The barrels of their guns are squeezed between their thighs. We're frightened, but we all want to see our killers.

Being female meant she could go places male journalists couldn't, especially among conservative Chechen women, who wouldn't talk to a male stranger. Among other things, this allowed her to write about the routine use of rape by Russian security personnel. "The very fact that I'm just a civilian gives me that much deeper an understanding of the experiences of other such civilians, living in Chechen towns and villages, who are caught in the war."

Embarrassed by the coverage, Russian authorities directly threatened Politkovskaya. They hoped she'd stop traveling to the province and writing about what she saw. In one village, Russian soldiers beat her, then threatened her with rape and execution. "The lieutenant colonel was very happy when I crouched in fright," she wrote.

Politkovskaya traveled outside Russia constantly to talk about what she was covering in Chechnya, hoping that the international community would do something to stop the carnage. It was grueling, frustrating work. "The world capitals flash before my eyes as I campaign for support," she wrote. "This spring I've been in Amsterdam, Paris, Geneva, Manila, Bonn, Hamburg. . . . Everywhere they invite me to make a speech about 'the situation in Chechnya,' but there are zero results."

At the same time, the Russians knew Politkovskaya had an access and credibility that was unmatched. In 2002 Chechen rebels seized 912 hostages in a Moscow theater during a performance of a musical. They asked Politkovskaya to negotiate a peaceful resolution, which failed. Russian special forces stormed the building after laying down a cloud of gas. Thirty-three Chechens and 130 hostages died. Russia used the siege to crack down on press freedom, meaning that reporting was harder than ever.

She knew that she didn't have to travel to a war zone to be in danger. On a flight in 2004 Politkovskaya lost consciousness after drinking a cup of tea and woke up hours later in a hospital. A nurse whispered to her, "My dear, they tried to poison you," she later wrote, meaning the Russian state.

On October 7, 2006, neighbors found Politkovskaya shot twice in the elevator of her apartment block. She'd been working on a story about torture by Chechen security force members working with the Russians. Later, Russian police seized her notes, computer, and photographs. At the time of her death, she had two children and was about to become a grandmother.

REPORTERS IN RUSSIA

Russia remains one of the most dangerous countries in the world for journalists. Since Vladimir Putin came to power in 2000, dozens of journalists have been killed in suspicious circumstances. Russian operatives have also been linked to multiple cases of the poisoning of dissidents and journalists.

A year later, police arrested several suspected Chechen gangsters and former Russian intelligence service agents in connection with her murder. After several proceedings, in 2014 a Russian court sentenced six men. However, rights groups pointed out that the people who ordered and planned it remain free, part of a broader trend of impunity for those who kill Putin's critics.

Unfortunately, while Chechnya has rebuilt, the area remains violent. Akhmat Kadyrov, a rebel leader, switched sides in 1999 to join the Russians and helped them brutally quell the independence movement he'd once supported. In 2004 Islamic fundamentalists hid a bomb at an event where he was speaking, killing him and 30 others. His equally brutal son, Ramzan, had Russia's backing to become president. He imposed a brutal dictatorship, killing political opponents and launching a campaign of torture of gay men.

While Politkovskaya knew things could always get worse, she never quelled her own conviction that people had the power to make things better. "Now, you have to believe in luck," she once told a friend. "We're nothing without it."

DISCUSSION QUESTIONS

1. Can you think of examples of activists or journalists being harmed or imprisoned for what they believe? What can the international community do to help them?

2. Are there news stories that are difficult for you to listen to because of the violent or disturbing details? A journalist's job is to bring vivid details to you so you can decide your own position on an issue. But how can journalists manage information that is difficult for many to absorb?

3. Do you feel less empathy for civilians in countries viewed as enemies or aggressors? Do cultural attitudes and the significant popular support for brutal, autocratic regimes lessen your desire to stand up for rights in those places?

THE ACCIDENTAL ENVIRONMENTALIST: CATHERINE COLEMAN FLOWERS

⚑ THE FIGHT AGAINST ENVIRONMENTAL RACISM

👤 1958–

📍 UNITED STATES

Choose a problem, decide what to focus on, and you will see results.

In summer, fields in Lowndes County, Alabama, roast under a relentless sun. The sweet smell of grass and goldenrod swirl with the funk of country-road asphalt.

But around many homes, the smell is anything but pleasant. In many areas, raw sewage gushes directly into yards dotted with children's toys. Dense clouds of flies hover. In the stinking mud lurk microscopic parasites.

The reason is as simple as it is shocking. The clay-rich soil is too dense for normal septic tanks. Many people live beyond city sewage systems and can't afford to install their own. Even the systems that are installed often don't work properly. The government prefers to turn a blind eye to the mainly poor, Black residents.

So raw sewage—dishwater, bath water, feces, and urine—either backs up into the houses or drains directly into yards.

For many, moving isn't an option because they live paycheck to paycheck or are on fixed incomes. Jobs that pay well are scarce, as few companies will do business in Lowndes County, where there's limited access to basic services like sewage treatment. Today, Lowndes is one of the poorest counties in one of America's poorest states. And it's been that way for as long as Catherine Coleman Flowers can remember.

Flowers grew up in the tiny Lowdnes community of Blackbelt. Black Belt is also the name of a 30-mile-wide curve of black dirt that starts in eastern Virginia and extends through the Carolinas, Georgia, Alabama, and eastern Texas. Plantation owners realized the soil was perfect for cotton. To till it, they brought enslaved Black men, women, and children. Black Belt also refers to the history of African American settlement in this region after the Civil War and emancipation.

As a child, Flowers reveled in her community, which centered on porches and a neighborhood well. Her parents were activists. Blackbelt lies between the civil rights hot spots of Selma and Montgomery, so civil rights activists came to their porch for fellowship and long strategy sessions. Among them was Stokely Carmichael, chair of the Student Nonviolent Coordinating Committee, a student-led civil rights group. "At the time, I did not realize I was not among common men," Flowers later wrote in her memoir, *Waste*.

With her father's support, Flowers led successful protests to improve education in her high school. In college, she stopped a proposed merger between her historically Black college and a White college, since she believed this would cut off an important way for Black people to get an education.

As a young person, she learned that there was no single way to create change. Drawing attention to a problem was a vital step. So was persistence and prayer. She soon learned that she'd been born into a system "that was designed to be against me." Her faith, she says, grew "stronger through adversity."

THE BLACK PANTHER PARTY

While in Lowndes, Stokely Carmichael helped form the Lowndes County Freedom Organization, an all-Black group that later helped inspire the Black Panther Party.

Carmichael, who later changed his name to Kwame Ture, was impatient with Dr. Martin Luther King Jr.'s strategy of raising moral awareness. Carmichael chose to focus on winning Black power through local organizing and elections. Bobby Seale and Huey P. Newton organized the Oakland, California–based Black Panther Party in 1966.

A family tragedy presented her with a new problem. After she married, her husband, an Army officer, suffered a head injury. When she took him home from the hospital, she realized he had amnesia—and no idea who she was. She became an activist caregiver because the military refused to treat him for memory loss. She barreled all the way up the chain of command until he was treated properly. "My life's experiences up to that point had taught me that looking the other way often led to more injustice."

SEPTIC TANKS

A septic tank is installed underground to collect household waste, including urine and feces. Most septic tanks function by breaking down waste and draining the leftover fluid into the surrounding dirt.

In Lowndes, however, the clay-rich soil doesn't drain well. New hybrid systems that provide additional filtration may help, though they are expensive and would require government investment to install.

Flowers completed a master's degree and began teaching school in Washington, DC, then in North Carolina, where she, her husband, and their infant daughter moved to be closer to family. A familiar pattern emerged. Everywhere Flowers went, she couldn't stop seeing injustice and doing something about it. Her Black students weren't expected to succeed, she realized. She wanted to inspire them, so she brought activists and Black leaders into the classroom to talk about how they made change.

But administrators accused her of "teaching students how to break the law." Believing that the system discriminated against her North Carolina students, she filed a federal civil rights complaint. Eventually, the schools had to demonstrate how they planned to address discrimination. As she wrote in *Waste*, she was "the first teacher in the history of the US Department of Education to file a federal civil rights complaint on behalf of students."

But Lowndes kept pulling her back. "Go to any cemetery in this county and you'll see the graves of my people," she wrote. "I sense their blood and sweat in this fertile soil."

When Flowers realizes someone might be able to help her, she's not shy in reaching out. She felt energized but also overwhelmed. People needed jobs in Lowndes, but companies weren't moving to the area because of a lack of crucial infrastructure, like sewage systems and the Internet. People who'd lived there for generations still lacked basic services, a challenge faced by many people living in rural areas.

A new lesson Flowers learned was not letting partisan politics limit whom she'd ask to help. Some were Republicans. Others were Democrats or independents. She also learned that there's nothing more powerful than bringing people to see the problem for themselves—especially the stinky one in so many Lowndes yards.

One of the first delegations she brought to Lowndes came across a local pastor in tears. He'd had to close the church because it lacked a septic system. Like other residents, he'd also been threatened with arrest if he didn't spend thousands of dollars the congregation didn't have to install it.

The same problem appeared in house after house. Flowers documented not only how the lack of adequate sewage damaged the environment but also how it damaged people. She convinced Baylor University to do a study. The study revealed that some Lowndes residents have hookworm, a parasite thought to be mostly eradicated in America. Hookworm is among the diseases, like cholera, strongly related to poverty.

She also knows that the problem was much bigger than raw sewage—for Flowers, Lowndes was the eye of a virtual hurricane of racism, poverty, and government neglect. Flowers is among a growing group of international rights activists who trace a close connection between racism, the environment, climate change, and human rights. Like Berta Cáceres, who fought hydropower plants in Honduras (discussed in the chapter "Sacred Rivers"), Flowers talks frequently about how communities of color around the world are targeted by polluters and neglected by government.

A term for this is *environmental racism*, which recognizes that a disproportionate number of people who live in environmentally hazardous areas are either people of color or poor. These communities also face the brunt of climate change with increased flooding, drought, and temperature extremes.

For Flowers, human rights don't just give her a framework to demand justice. The mechanisms of international human rights institutions and courts provide a tool to get governments to act.

Flowers raised money to create nongovernmental organizations to work on the intersecting challenges of health, economic disparities, and access to clean air, water, and soil in marginalized rural communities. In 2018 Flowers partnered with Earthjustice, which specializes in environmental law, to file a federal Civil Rights Act complaint against the Alabama Department of Public Health and the Lowndes County Health

Department for the failing to improve wastewater treatment, causing a "disproportionate and adverse effect" on the Black community.

HOOKWORM

Ancylostoma duodenale, Ancylostoma ceylanicum, and *Necator americanus* are commonly known as hookworms. Their lifecycle starts in the small intestine of an infected person. The worms lay eggs that pass out in feces, then hatch into immature worms, or larvae.

After some time, the larvae use their jagged teeth to dig into human skin, mainly through the sole of the foot, then pass through the bloodstream back into the intestine, where the lifecycle repeats.

Flowers is willing to take her message anywhere. During the 2020 US presidential campaign, she brought Democratic candidates US Senator Cory Booker (D-NJ) and US Senator Bernie Sanders (D-VT) to Lowndes. She also worked hard to draw international attention, succeeding in bringing to Lowndes the UN special rapporteur on extreme poverty and human rights. After visiting, the rapporteur was so shocked, all he could say was, "This is not a sight that one normally sees" in developed countries.

One of the people she introduced visitors to was her friend, Pamela Rush. Rush lived with two children in a dilapidated trailer in a polluted yard. To keep out vermin, Rush stuffed rags into holes in the walls. Like many Black families, Rush also faced financial discrimination. To buy the trailer, she'd borrowed money from a bank. But the bank charged a high interest rate, meaning that she'd paid the trailer's initial cost but still owed thousands of dollars.

One supporter offered to purchase a safe, clean trailer for Rush. But paying for a new septic system was well beyond her means. Then the coronavirus pandemic struck. In Alabama, Black people were twice as likely as their White neighbors to die from COVID-19. Rush got sick and died in 2020 at age 49, before she could move into a new trailer.

Flowers points out that it took courage for Rush to speak out and invite others in. "She opened her private world to the public to expose what poverty really looks like. Now they have a face—they've seen it. It's not something you can get out of your mind."

In 2020 Flowers won a prestigious MacArthur "genius" fellowship award, which she's invested back into her work. Flowers is quick to point out that poor sanitation goes well beyond one town or even one country. The inequities she's uncovered in Lowndes speak to a larger threat everyone faces: the contamination of our planet and climate change.

Flowers is willing to travel anywhere to talk about creating action on environmental justice and climate change. In 2016 she visited the Standing Rock protests of the Dakota Access Pipeline, built to carry crude oil from Canada to US-based refineries. Indigenous communities stood in the way of construction because the pipeline risked contaminating ancestral lands and rivers.

Flowers listened as protesters talked about how their ancestors believed they had to work to protect the earth for the next seven generations. "Earth is our common home," she says. "I want to make sure that I make a difference that can impact seven generations to come."

DISCUSSION QUESTIONS

1. Flowers fought to stop a merger between her historically Black college—one of the HBCUs, or historically Black colleges and universities—and a White college. How might such a merger reduce educational opportunities for Black students despite the larger college's access to resources? What is the historical reason for having Black-identified colleges?

2. "There's nothing like bringing people to Lowndes and not only having them smell the stench," Flowers says. What other poverty conditions might a politician want to change after living in it for a day? Have you visited a place and thought you would not be able to live in those conditions?

3. Banks charge interest on money people borrow as loans. That means the bank makes a percentage of each dollar it lends. A loan allows the borrower to buy things they couldn't otherwise afford, like a house, land, or a car. Historically in America, lenders have either refused to lend Black people money or have charged them higher interest rates than White people. Why do you think this happens? What problems does this create? Do you think this is a human rights issue?

SACRED RIVERS: BERTA CÁCERES

⚑ FIGHTING FOR THE ENVIRONMENT
👤 1971–2016
📍 HONDURAS

> *They are afraid of us because we are not afraid of them.*

Lenca elders taught Berta Cáceres that her people grew from the land, corn, and water. Rivers are sacred. The Lenca were meant to be the rivers' guardians "for the good of humanity and this planet," Berta often said.

In modern-day Honduras, Lenca women wear bright headscarves and blouses bordered in hand-crocheted lace. Men wear cowboy hats, their faces leathered by hard work and sun. Many families still cook over wood fires and live far from roads.

The strongest influence on Cáceres was her mother. Mama Berta had 11 children but always managed to help others. Women would make the hike, often lasting days, from their farms to the town of La Esperanza so that Mama Berta could deliver their babies or treat their children. Cáceres helped her mother by fetching medication, helping deliver babies, or just lighting candles. Mama Berta also served as mayor La Esperanza and as an elected member of the Honduran Congress.

The Honduran and American governments have historically been closely allied and often coordinate their polices. That hasn't been good for the Honduran people, Cáceres came to believe. In the 1800s, American investors built plantations to grow fruit, especially bananas, then built roads and railroads to ship the fruit to America—not help the Honduran people.

THE LENCA

The Lenca are Honduras's largest group of Indigenous people. There are approximately 100,000 Lenca in Honduras and 37,000 in El Salvador.

The Lenca lived between the ruins of great empires: the Maya to the north and the Chibcha and Inca to the south. The Lenca had their own language and customs, and they traded with other Indigenous groups like the Maya Ch'ortí and the Pech.

When she went away to college, Cáceres brought her mother's sense of justice with her. She knew that taking action was the only way to make change. Cáceres helped found the Civic Council of Popular and Indigenous Organizations of Honduras (COPINH) in 1993. The group represents over 200 Indigenous Honduran communities.

Cáceres got busy organizing. She hoped to bring human rights to Honduras. At first, she tried to work with the country's leaders. Along with the Lenca, Honduras's largest Indigenous group, Cáceres made common cause with the Garífuna, a community descended from African enslaved people.

But in 2009 the Honduran military seized power. The generals approved the construction of dozens of dams, mines, and biofuel plantations, many located on Indigenous lands. They did this without asking Indigenous people for permission. A "David versus Goliath battle for water" started, one reporter wrote. Unless the people could stop it, the Honduran government was going to "[sell] off the country's rivers and other natural resources to the highest bidders."

HONDURAS

When Christopher Columbus first saw Honduras's Atlantic coast, he named the place for its deep (*hondo*) waters. The Spanish invaded in 1524, setting off a violent scramble for the country's natural resources. Some Indigenous people resisted while others were enslaved.

No project was more controversial than Agua Zarca. When completed, the Agua Zarca dam would block the Gualcarque River, sacred to the Lenca. In March 2013, locals spotted "no entry" signs on their own lands. Armed security guards even stopped them from drawing water to drink, clean, and cook. Bulldozers pushed down trees and built roads.

How would the trees and native animals find water to drink if it was all taken by the dam, Cáceres wondered. *What would happen to the fish that Lenca people eat?*

Berta and COPINH launched a protest. The government responded by sending in soldiers. Berta quickly realized that the problem was bigger than Honduras. The government had American support. The US Congress gave Honduras's corrupt government money to fund the military and make it into a kind of police force. It didn't seem to matter that the soldiers attacked peaceful Honduran citizens.

The Honduran government tried to bribe Cáceres and other COPINH leaders to be quiet. When they refused, the government sent more soldiers. She organized blockades of the roads leading to the dam construction sites. In July 2013 the Honduran military killed one protester and injured three others. The protester's son later told journalists, "We were protesting peacefully but they killed my father. Our lives are so much worse without him, I want the soldier to face the full weight of the law because he didn't kill an animal. He killed a human."

The following year, the human rights group Global Witness called Honduras the most dangerous country in the world for activists working to defend Indigenous people's right to land. Between 2002 and 2014, the group registered the murders of 111 human rights defenders, 12 in 2014 alone.

Cáceres wouldn't give up. "The Gualcarque River has called upon us as have other gravely threatened rivers," she said. "We must answer their call."

Some investors got cold feet and withdrew support for Agua Zarca. But Desarrollos Energéticos (DESA) remained. DESA is controlled by a powerful Honduran family suspected of having backed the 2009 coup.

An investigation by the Sierra Club found a close relationship between DESA and the Honduran military.

DESA moved construction to another place to avoid the blockade. Officials filed false charges against Cáceres and other leaders. DESA tried to get Lenca families arrested for trespassing, even though these families were in their own communities and farms.

Cáceres and COPINH's work drew international attention. "It is clear that Berta Cáceres is being harassed to stop her from defending the rights of the Lenca people," Amnesty International said.

BANANA REPUBLIC

US involvement in Honduras gave rise to the term *banana republic*. A banana republic means a politically unstable country ruled by dictators and where corporations can do what they want.

Cáceres knew her life was in danger. She'd been told her name was at the top of a death list of 17 other human rights leaders. By then, she had four children. Often, she slept in friends' houses. She never traveled alone, to elude any attackers. "I want to live, there are many things I still want to do in this world but I have never once considered giving up fighting for our territory, for a life with dignity, because our fight is legitimate. I take lots of care, but in the end, in this country where there is total impunity, I am vulnerable. . . . When they want to kill me, they will do it."

Along with her environmental work, Cáceres was a committed feminist, antiracist, and supporter of gay rights. The one thing she refused to do was stop protesting. "They are afraid of us because we are not afraid of them," she said.

In 2015 Cáceres was awarded the prestigious Goldman Environmental Prize. The prize is like the Nobel Peace Prize but for environmentalists. Journalists and activists flocked to La Esperanza to interview her. She said, "It's a very difficult situation. I cannot freely walk on my territory or swim in the sacred river and I am separated from my children because of the threats. I cannot live in peace. I am always thinking about being killed or kidnapped. But I do not want to leave my country. I refuse to go into exile. I am a human rights fighter and I will not give up this fight."

Cáceres and COPINH founded a women's health center, five Indigenous radio stations, and an activism training and retreat center in La Esperanza. "The whole world admired her," Mama Berta told the Sierra Club. "She traveled abroad to help, to give trainings, to give talks, and to carry the message of what was happening here. She had this immense ability to defeat, a little bit, the huge power of the businesses and the big landowners that were her enemy."

Even though everyone knew Cáceres's life was in danger, Honduras did nothing to protect her. No one was guarding her La Esperanza home when armed men burst in on March 2, 2016, and killed her. Cáceres was 44.

A year later, a Honduran court convicted seven men for her murder. Although the trial was flawed, the court did reveal evidence that a DESA executive hired assassins to kill Cáceres. The company president—who has denied wrongdoing—had even befriended Cáceres as a way of getting information about her whereabouts. He was later convicted for his role in her murder.

Honduras remains mired in corruption and violence. Although Agua Zarca was never completed, other projects continue to be built without any consultation with local communities. The capital, Tegucigalpa, is torn apart by violence linked to the trade in illegal drugs, most of which are consumed in the United States.

Yet many human rights activists continue to do Cáceres' work. One of them is her daughter, Bertita. Just as her mother looked to Mama Berta for inspiration, so does Bertita look to her mother. "If it was an isolated struggle—if it was just the struggle of me, or my mother, or COPINH—it would be very sad," Bertita has said. "But when you see the collective struggle, when you see that it's not just the Lenca people, it's all across Honduras and beyond—that's where I see my mother, that's where I feel her presence, and that's where I'm really filled with hope."

DISCUSSION QUESTIONS

1. The United States provides military and humanitarian aid to many countries. Do you support this and why? What if that country has a pattern of human rights abuses?

2. Many of the refugees trying to cross the US border with Mexico are fleeing violence in Honduras. Much of that violence stems from the illegal trade in narcotics, most sent to American consumers. Does the United States have a special responsibility

to help Honduran refugees? How might governments reduce human rights abuses stemming from the drug trade?

3. Why do you think AM and FM radio stations are so important in rural areas in poor countries?

THE TIGRESS:
FANNYANN EDDY

🏴 **THE RIGHTS OF LGBTQ PEOPLE**

👤 **1974-2004**

📍 **SIERRA LEONE**

Silence creates vulnerability.

When FannyAnn Eddy stood to speak at the April 2004 meeting of the United Nations Commission on Human Rights, few could have guessed at the route that led her to that podium. For 10 years, she'd been a refugee, after fleeing a horrific war in her native Sierra Leone. Before then, she'd been homeless, rejected by her own family because she was a lesbian.

A slight, slender woman with a close-cropped haircut, Eddy came off as shy in a crowd. But the minute she stepped to a podium, her voice was strong and assured. "We called her 'the Tigress,'" one friend said fondly, not only because she fiercely protected her LGBTQ friends. "It was also for her determination to support her causes and talk frankly."

Eddy was in Geneva, Switzerland, to support the Brazilian Resolution, a step to formally declare sexual orientation a human right. The commission is the part of the United Nations where member states draft new human rights agreements. Championed by the Brazilian government and supported by over a dozen nations, Brazil led this effort to make violence and discrimination against people solely because of their sexual orientation a clear violation of human rights.

BLOOD DIAMONDS

A fight over natural resources helped spur Sierra Leone's war. Among the resources were blood diamonds, also called conflict diamonds. Mined in conflict areas, often with forced labor, the stones are then sold with the profits going in part to fund more violence.

In 2003 the international community established the Kimberley Process to prevent many blood diamonds from being sold. This involves a certification for uncut diamonds that are mined legally. Governments can seize uncertified stones and prosecute illegal vendors. While more needs to be done, the certification has significantly reduced any incentive to market blood diamonds.

Eddy wanted to help "break the silence," in her words, that covered up abuses against the LGBTQ communities. She was especially proud to speak as an African. Gay rights weren't just an issue for the United States and Europe; she wanted the international community to understand. Gay Africans also wanted equal rights.

Yet "many African leaders do not want to even acknowledge that we exist," she said to the commission. "Their denial has many disastrous results for our community. We do exist. But because of the denial of our existence, we live in constant fear: fear of the police and officials with the power to arrest and detain us simply because of our sexual orientation."

Eddy spoke from hard experience. When she came out to her family in the Sierra Leone capital of Freetown, they kicked her out. When she was just 17, a different disaster struck. Rebels attempted to violently overthrow Sierra Leone's government. The rebellion was supported by ruthless Liberian rebel leader and later president, Charles Taylor, who provided money and weapons. All sides in Sierra Leone's conflict—the rebels, the army, and ethnic progovernment militias—responded brutally, plunging the country into a war that lasted for 11 years.

THE UN SPECIAL COURT FOR SIERRA LEONE

In 2012 the UN Special Court for Sierra Leone convicted Charles Taylor for crimes against humanity and war crimes, sentencing him to 50 years in prison. Prosecutors sought to highlight cases involving violence against women and children, many of whom were forcibly recruited as soldiers. Taylor was the first former head of state to be convicted by an international tribunal since Nuremberg. At the time of this writing, he continues to serve his sentence at a prison in the United Kingdom.

The war took violence to new levels. Rebels perpetrated hundreds of massacres. Fighters raped, stole, and forcibly amputated people's limbs to demonstrate their total power.

Mutilations have a long history in African colonies, including in what was the Belgian Congo. There, workers who failed to deliver a set quota of raw rubber to European companies could be killed. Companies required proof of the killings with severed hands.

All sides in Sierra Leone's war executed suspected enemies and destroyed villages. Tens of thousands of people died before the warring groups signed peace accords in 2002.

During this time, almost half of all Sierra Leonians fled the country as refugees, Eddy among them. For a time, she stayed in neighboring Guinea, then Zimbabwe. But her escape brought an unexpected benefit. Like Sierra Leone, Zimbabwe bans same-sex marriage and allows discrimination. But Eddy befriended Zimbabwean gay people who organized to fight for their rights. She saw how gay people were living more openly and speaking out.

Eddy considered settling permanently outside Sierra Leone. She wanted to make a life for herself, her son, and her partner. But she realized she couldn't abandon the fight for human rights within her own country. Sierra Leone should not just rebuild from the devastation of war, she believed. With other Sierra Leoneans, she wanted to build a country where gay people had the same rights as everyone else.

"This is my country, and people have to change it," she once told a friend. "God needs human hands to do this work. Gay people have the right to be protected by their government and to have freedom."

Hudson Tucker remembers meeting Eddy on a Freetown beach soon after she returned in 1991. Sierra Leone is a tropical country, with warm temperatures year-round and miles of sandy beaches. Over the rasp of waves and sips of palm wine, Tucker and Eddy became close friends. They started the Sierra Leone Lesbian and Gay Association (SLLAGA), the first public group in the country to defend gay rights. SLLAGA began reporting on cases of discrimination and attacks against LGBTQ people and publicly opposed homophobic and transphobic laws. SLLAGA also provided social and mental health support to LGBTQ Sierra Leoneans.

The work was hard. Due to widespread fearmongering by politicians, many Africans view homosexuality as sinful and un-African. The vast majority of African laws that discriminate against gay people were written by European colonial powers. Some precolonial African cultures accepted same-sex relations, a spectrum of gender identities, and even marriage between same-sex people. In what is now modern Benin, to the east of Sierra Leone, kings had female armies, challenging contemporary Western gender roles. Women leaders and healers could have same-sex marriage or engage in polygyny, or marriage with multiple women.

Yet in most of today's Africa, being identified as gay can be dangerous. In Somalia, for example, gay men can be executed just because they are gay. In Uganda, courts can sentence gay men to life sentences for having consensual sex with other men. Nigeria makes it illegal for anyone to officiate at a same-sex wedding or officially register a gay club or organization, punishable by up to 10 years in jail.

Women don't face similar punishment in African countries but can legally be fired because of their sexual orientation. Perpetrators of violence are rarely punished. Even in Freetown, SLLAGA couldn't rent its own office due to the threat that the office would be attacked. Also, gay

Sierra Leoneans feared being seen in an office linked to an LGBTQ rights group, knowing they could be outed to their families or employers.

Instead, Eddy borrowed the offices of other groups at night, after the staff had left for the day. Her work extended beyond Sierra Leone after she joined the All Africa Rights Initiative and the Coalition of African Lesbians.

UN STATEMENTS

A formal statement or resolution from the UN may seem like a small advance (and in some ways, it is). For LGBTQ communities, the wait for strong support of their rights has been frustrating as well as dangerous for their lives.

But these documents are essential building blocks for a world consensus on defining, implementing, and protecting human rights. The documents provide a mechanism—painfully slow, to be sure—to create not only laws but also understanding among diverse communities for what it means to be human.

Her friends worried about her safety. Eddy refused to hide her identity and lived openly with her female partner. She never minced words, one friend said, even though this meant that she regularly received threats. Once, flyers appeared in front of her home with the words KILL THE GAYS.

Eddy also worked on another issue facing Sierra Leone and the rest of the world: AIDS. Many Sierra Leoneans lacked basic sex education, fueling the spread of HIV. Also, threats against LGBTQ people meant that many hid their symptoms or never got tested for fear of being shunned.

In 2002 Eddy and other SLLAGA members traveled to South Africa. There, activists were fighting to legalize gay marriage (they won in 2006). Cities like Johannesburg and Cape Town had thriving gay neighborhoods and businesses. One friend recalled realizing that the treatment they took for granted in Sierra Leone, like being fired for being gay, could get the employer punished in South Africa. Though they knew this would mean years of work, Eddy and the other SLLAGA members wanted human rights for gay Sierra Leoneans—and the rest of Africa.

Several months after Eddy returned to Freetown, a former SLLAGA employee broke into her home, which also served as the organization's office. Authorities suspect that he raped and murdered Eddy. Although the man was briefly detained for her murder, he later escaped. No one has been convicted of her murder, which many believe was in part motivated by her sexuality.

Homosexuality remains against the law in 34 of Africa's 54 countries. Few LGBTQ people can live openly with partners, marry, or have legal custody of their children. People still fear being ostracized from their families or being fired from jobs just for being gay.

The Brazilian Resolution Eddy helped promote never passed. But there has been notable international progress. In 2015 12 UN agencies called for an end to violence and discrimination against adults, adolescents, and children who are lesbian, gay, bisexual, transgender, or intersex. The agencies also set out specific steps to protect these individuals. This was the first time that so many organizations within the United Nations membership joined forces in defense of these rights. As of this writing, at least three more resolutions defending LGBTQ rights have been approved at the UN, an important advance. It's not enough but is a sign that Eddy's fight continues.

In Sierra Leone, things are slowly changing for the better. "I can walk down the street with confidence and not worry that someone will spit in my face," one gay activist said in 2021. "People can dress as they like when they go to the beach. The younger people are more tolerant."

Eddy's group, SLLAGA, evolved into a new group called Dignity Association, which continues to work for gay rights. Dignity is not alone. The Freetown-based Concerned Women's Initiative also advocates for lesbian woman and girls. Eddy's friends believe the Tigress's work was not in vain. "FannyAnn was the light that opened the eyes of people in Sierra Leone to gays and lesbians. Because of her, you can no longer just push us aside."

DISCUSSION QUESTIONS

1. Some precolonial African cultures accepted fluid gender categories. Why might contemporary nations claim that being gay or transgender are at odds with African culture?

2. If you lived in fear because of your gender identity, would you choose to stay and fight for change, or would you choose to move to a place where your identity is accepted and celebrated?

3. Are you a "diplomat" or an "activist"? Would you rather negotiate or demand? What are the advantages and disadvantages of each strategy?

ACKNOWLEDGMENTS

My heartfelt thanks to the heroes who shared their stories directly with me: Judy Heumann, Ingrid Newkirk, Jody Williams, S. James Anaya, and Catherine Coleman Flowers. I'm also thankful to their staff for ably fielding follow-up questions and drafts. The librarians at Duke University sustained me through dozens of masked pickup and drop-off appointments as I sought to know better the heroes whose legacies form the durable supports of ongoing human rights advocacy. I love librarians!

Typical of human rights advocacy and writing, I counted on the help of many advocates and scholars in the effort to ensure the breadth and accuracy of these stories: Jo Becker, Cath Collins, Shellac Davies, Corinne Dufka, Filip Ericsson, Bill Frelick, Behrooz Ghamari-Tabrizi, Katalina Hadfield, Charles Henry, Danny Hoffman, Kyle Knight, Barbara Lau, Claudia Koonz, Hudson Tucker, Sumathi Ramaswamy, Frachele Scott, Dorothy Thomas, and Arpita Varghese.

A number of writer friends listened to, read, discussed, and offered both wise advice and constructive critique as this book took shape: Jenn Barnes, Anne Bowen, Kelly Dyksterhouse, Alison Jones, Rick Mashburn, Joe Neff, and Cynthia Surrisi.

I'm especially grateful to Elizabeth Partridge for her wisdom about writing nonfiction for children and young adults. She is a mentor to so many for her important and moving books. She encouraged my idea at the Loon Song writing retreat in northern Minnesota, helping to launch my journey.

My daughter, Frances D. Starn, inspires me daily with her dedication to teaching and to her students at Durham's Hillside High School (I feel the Hornets' immortal sting!). She pushed me to dig deeper in telling the stories of these individuals. I hope that some of her brilliance shines through in the writing.

Erin Regan and Elliott Regan O'Brien provided many hours of research and review to these chapters and helped me craft the discussion questions and sites to visit. I am indebted to both of them for helping to expand what was possible.

Ana Copenicker's illustrations bring me joy every time I see them.

The team at Chicago Review Press was a joy to work with. As the acquiring editor, Kara Rota ably and patiently shepherded the draft through several revisions. Frances Giguette offered a steady hand and inventive heart to the production process. Thank you also to Sadie Teper for the interior design; Joseph Webb for the copyedit; Allison Felus for the production management; marketing lead Jen DePoorter; and Alayna Parsons-Valles, editorial assistant.

Jacqui Lipton, my agent and a fellow writer, combines honesty with vision and a sense of the possible that I value and am grateful for every day.

As always, my work is sustained by colleagues, family, and friends. Adam Versényi remains a supportive partner, with loving words, meals, and (above all) a patient, perceptive ear.

My children, Frances and Ray, will always be extra miracles that inspire and lift me. I hope I've done something to create a better world for them and all of the world's children to come.

WHAT CAN I DO?

The heroes in this book come from different places, times, and backgrounds. But they share one important trait. They saw an injustice and decided to do something about it. You can use this page to think about an injustice you care about. Decide how you will learn more about it, find out who else cares about it, and begin to make a plan to make change for the better.

What injustice do I care about?

What people or groups work on this issue?

What do they say should be changed to protect human rights?

What do I think should be changed to protect human rights?

Who has the power to make those changes?

What is the best way to communicate to those with the power to make

changes?

Who can help me by amplifying my voice?

What would the world look like if those changes were made?

Please make a copy of this worksheet to fill it out for yourself.

SITES TO VISIT

DUNANT

Located in Solferino, Italy, the Museo Storico Risorgimentale focuses on Italian military history from 1796 to 1870. The nearby church of San Pietro features an ossuary that contains the bones of at least 7,000 men who were killed that fateful day. https://www.solferinoesanmartino.it/.

An International Committee of the Red Cross monument is located in Solferino: http://gardatourism.it/en/red-cross-memorial/.

Geneva, Switzerland, features an International Red Cross and Red Crescent Museum: https://www.redcrossmuseum.ch.

The League of Nations was based in the Palais des Nations in Geneva, Switzerland. The current United Nations Office, the second largest after the United Nations Headquarters in New York, is currently located there. Guided tours are available: https://www.ungeneva.org/en/about /palais-des-nations.

NANSEN

Nansen's polar exploits are the focus of the Fram Museum in Norway. The museum also includes material on other explorers, Roald Amundsen among them: https://frammuseum.no/.

The Museum of Political History of Russia in St. Petersburg includes photographs and other primary sources related to famine and relief efforts: https://polithistory.ru/en.

The State Central Museum of Contemporary History of Russia in Moscow also contains material on Russian famines: https://www.sovr history.ru/?lang=en.

The Nobel Prize Museum in Stockholm, Sweden, includes all the Nobel laureates mentioned in this book: https://www.nobelprize.org/about /nobel-museum.

The Armenian Genocide Museum-Institute in Yerevan, Armenia, is a moving memorial to the 20th century's first genocide: http://www .genocide-museum.am/eng/index.php.

JEBB

The Marlborough Library, where Jebb taught the children of St. Peter's School from 1899 to 1900, features a plaque commemorating Eglantyne Jebb. The library is located in Marlborough, Wiltshire.

Ellsmere College in Shropshire County, United Kingdom, installed a Jebb memorial garden to honor Eglantyne and her sister, Dorothy. The garden includes two sculptures and a labyrinth: https://www.ellesmere sculpture.co.uk/the-ellesmere-sculpture-trail.

Countries engaged in fighting during World War I erected many memorials, including this one in Washington, DC: https://www.worldwar1 centennial.org/index.php.

Many of the World War I battlefields have associated museums and walking tours like this one in Belgium: http://www.greatwar.co.uk/places /ypres-salient-battle-remains.htm.

CHANG

The Memorial Hall of the Boxer Rebellion, or Lvzu Memorial Hall in Tianjin, China, is open to visitors.

The Memorial Hall of the Victims in Nanjing Massacre by Japanese Invaders, located in Nanjing, China, has many photographs and artifacts.

More information is available here: https://www.chinesehistorydigest
.com/historic-sights/nanjing-massacre/memorial-hall-museum.

The Memorial Hall of the Chinese People's War of Resistance Against Japanese Aggression in Beijing, China, has a unique and extensive collection: https://www.trip.com/travel-guide/attraction/beijing/museum-of-the -war-of-chinese-people-s-resistance-against-japanese-aggression-76667.

MEHTA

The Hansa Mehta Library is part of University of Baroda in Vadodara, India.

RÓMULO

The Freedom Memorial Museum is under construction in Manila, the Philippines: https://hrvvmemcom.gov.ph.

Located in Warrenton, Virginia, the Cold War Museum is built in a former top secret army signals-intelligence base used during World War II and the Cold War: https://coldwar.org.

BUNCHE

A stainless-steel obelisk honoring Ralph J. Bunche stands near the United Nations at First Avenue and 43rd Street: https://www.nycgovparks .org/parks/ralph-bunche-park/monuments/195. Howard University also has a Ralph J. Bunche International Affairs Center.

The Center for Peace and Conflict Studies at Wayne State University holds an annual Ralph Bunche Summer Institute for high school students from metro Detroit and the international border area. The conference focuses on conflict resolution, diversity, civil rights, negotiation, international affairs, and how to individually foster peace: https://law.wayne.edu/keith-center/programs/ralph-bunche.

There are many civil rights museums in the United States, including the National Civil Rights Museum at the Lorraine Motel in Memphis, Tennessee (https://www.civilrightsmuseum.org), and the International Civil Rights Center and Museum in Greensboro, North Carolina (https://www.sitinmovement.org/).

The Apartheid Museum in Johannesburg, South Africa, covers the history of apartheid: https://www.apartheidmuseum.org.

FERENCZ

To get a sense of what Ferencz's childhood was like, visit the Tenement Museum in New York City: https://www.tenement.org.

The site of the Nuremberg Trials is open to visitors: https://museums.nuernberg.de/memorium-nuremberg-trials/.

There are many Holocaust museums. It's also possible to visit several of the concentration camps:

United States Holocaust Memorial Museum (Washington, DC): https://www.ushmm.org.

Yad Vashem (Israel): https://www.yadvashem.org.

Auschwitz-Birkenau (Poland): http://auschwitz.org/en.

Buchenwald and Mittelbau-Dora: https://www.buchenwald.de/en/171.

MURRAY

The Pauli Murray Center for History and Social Justice is located in the former Fitzgerald family home in Durham, North Carolina: https://www.paulimurraycenter.com/.

JARA

Chile's Museum of Memory and Human Rights chronicles the dirty war and makes special mention of Jara and his music: https://web.museodelamemoria.cl/.

Villa Grimaldi is a former torture and execution site that contains a peace park: http://villagrimaldi.cl.

MÉNDEZ

The former location of the Argentine Navy Mechanics' School, is now a park devoted to human rights. It's possible to visit the attics where detainees were kept: http://www.museositioesma.gob.ar.

HEUMANN

A memorial honoring President Franklin Delano Roosevelt (and his Scottish terrier, Murray the Outlaw of Falahill, or Fala for short) is on the National Mall in Washington, DC. In one statue, FDR is depicted in a wheelchair. This memorial is the only US presidential memorial to depict a First Lady. In the last room of the memorial, the emblem of the United Nations hangs behind Eleanor Roosevelt, for her time chairing the UN Commission on Human Rights.

NEWKIRK

The PETA Museum of Tofu is set to open in New York City. According to PETA, the museum will include the world's largest silken-tofu wrestling pit and a café featuring tofu-based recipes.

WILLIAMS

The Hiroshima Peace Memorial Museum in Hiroshima, Japan, (http://hpmmuseum.jp) and the Nagasaki National Peace Memorial Hall for the Atomic Bomb Victims in Nagasaki, Japan, (https://www.peace-nagasaki.go.jp/en) house relics of the explosion as well as the first-hand testimony of survivors.

ANAYA

Two locations of the National Museum of the American Indian (in Washington, DC, and New York, NY) are curated primarily by Indigenous communities: https://americanindian.si.edu.

You can learn more about Deskaheh by attending the Annual Iroquois Arts Festival, which celebrates Haudenosaunee creativity with live performances by cultural groups, demonstrations, an outdoor arts market with traditional and contemporary arts and fine crafts, family activities, and more. In recent times, the celebration has been held in Howes Cave, New York.

After the US Army forced the Chiricahua Apaches to surrender, the US government sent families in cattle cars to Fort Pickens and Fort Marian in Florida. But the authorities separated out the children, some of whom were forced to attend the Carlisle Indian Industrial boarding school in Carlisle, Pennsylvania. The school opened in 1879 as the first government-run boarding school for Native American children. Soon followed by other boarding schools, Carlisle's goal was to force the assimilation of Native children into White American society by compelling them to speak only English and convert to Christianity. At Carlisle, over 150 died. The school closed in 1918. The Carlisle Indian Cemetery can be visited, and a new museum is being planned: https://carlisleindianschoolproject.com/.

Nearby Dickinson College maintains a digital project of the school records at http://carlisleindian.dickinson.edu.

Among the Carlisle alumni is Jim Thorpe, a member of the Sac and Fox Nation who went on to win gold medals in the 1912 Olympics and play professional baseball, basketball, and football. Thorpe's monument stands near the town named for him, Jim Thorpe, Pennsylvania. The grave rests on mounds of soil from Thorpe's native Oklahoma and from the stadium in which he won his Olympic medals.

The Sandinista Revolution Museum (Museo de la Revolución) is open for visitors in León, Nicaragua.

The Tiscapa Historical National Park in Managua, Nicaragua, chronicles some of the abuses that took place during the fight to topple the US-backed dictatorship: https://vianica.com/activitydetails/163/tiscapa-historical-national-park.

FLOWERS

The Equal Justice Initiative, which partners with Catherine Coleman Flowers, maintains two sites in Montgomery, Alabama: The National Memorial for Peace and Justice and the Legacy Museum, both open to visitors: https://museumandmemorial.eji.org/memorial.

The National Center for Civil and Human Rights in Atlanta chronicles the US civil rights movement: https://www.civilandhumanrights.org.

The Oakland Museum of California has a permanent Black Power exhibit that includes the Black Panthers: https://museumca.org/projects /black-power.

EDDY

The Sierra Leone Peace Museum in Freetown, Sierra Leone, is open for visitors: http://www.sierraleonetrc.org/index.php/sierra-leone-peace -museum.

The University of Victoria in Canada maintains Transgender Archives and online exhibits: https://www.uvic.ca/transgenderarchives.

The National Museum of American Diplomacy in Washington, DC, maintains a permanent Conflict Minerals exhibit: https://diplomacy .state.gov/exhibits/diplomacy-is-our-mission/conflict-minerals/.

GLOSSARY

AMERICAN CIVIL LIBERTIES UNION (ACLU): A nonprofit organization that protects people's civil rights in the United States.

AMNESTY INTERNATIONAL (AI): An international nongovernmental organization (NGO) and nonprofit organization that advocates for human rights through legal action and public campaigns.

APARTHEID: A system of racial partition applied with violence and discrimination in South Africa from 1948 to 1994.

ARBITRAMENT: The settling of a dispute by a mediator or judge.

ARCHIPELAGO: A cluster of islands in a body of water. Indonesia is the world's largest archipelago nation with more that 18,000 islands.

AUTOCRAT: A ruler with unlimited power and authority.

AYATOLLAH: The Shia term for a high-ranking cleric.

BIAS: An unfair or prejudicial favor or disfavor toward an idea or thing. This preference can be learned or innate.

BLOCKADE: The forced sealing of access to a place in an effort to cut off a supply of goods or communication.

BURKA (OR BURQA): Islamic women's garment that covers the entire body and includes a mesh panel over the eyes.

CASTE SYSTEM: A social class system determined by the family to which one is born.

CEREBRAL PALSY: A disorder caused by abnormal brain development that results in inability to move or retain posture.

CHADOR: A garment frequently used by women in Iran that includes a head covering and cloak that reaches to the feet.

CIVILIAN: A person who is not on active duty with a military, naval, police, or firefighting organization.

COLD WAR: In contrast to a "hot war" with battles, the Cold War is fought via secret means and with acts of aggression that fall short of armed conflict, such as propaganda, population and economic controls, espionage, and threats. The Cold War refers to the period starting with the end of World War II in 1945 and lasting until the fall of the Berlin Wall in 1989, followed by the breakup of the Soviet Union and the independence of Central and Eastern Europe.

EXTRADITION: The legal transfer of a detainee from the jurisdiction of one country to another.

EXTRAJUDICIAL: Outside the formal legal system.

FOREIGN DIRECT INVESTMENT: An investment in the form of controlling ownership (directing business practices versus owning shares) in a company entirely based in another country.

FUNDAMENTALISM: A version of an ideology or religion that is extreme or a strict, literal interpretation.

GADFLY: A person who agitates the status quo of a society with commentary or criticism.

GENEVA CONVENTIONS: The treaties and protocols that establish international standards for the humanitarian rules of war.

GENOCIDE: The deliberate and systematic destruction of a particular racial, ethnic, national, or political group.

HABEAS CORPUS: Literally "show me the body" in Latin. A legal protection against unlawful imprisonment where a person must be brought before a judge to determine the legality of that person's confinement.

HIJAB (ALSO SPELLED HEJAB): A woman's covering over the hair, neck, and shoulders.

HUMANISM: A philosophy outside of religion that emphasizes the agency and goodness of human beings as the basis for applying rational and ethical solutions to human welfare problems.

IMAM: A religious leadership position in both Sunni and Shia Islam.

IMPUNITY: Freedom from punishment or consequences for an action.

INDISCRIMINATE WEAPON: A weapon that cannot be aimed exclusively at a military target or be constrained as required under international humanitarian law. One example is the poison gas used by Germans, French, and British forces in World War I.

INTERNATIONAL CRIMINAL COURT (ICC): A permanent international body under the jurisdiction of the United Nations that investigates and prosecutes genocide, war crimes, and crimes against humanity. The ICC is located in The Hague, Netherlands.

INTERSECTIONALITY: The complex, cumulative way in which the effects of multiple forms of discrimination (such as racism, sexism, and classism) combine, overlap, or intersect especially in the experiences of marginalized individuals or groups.

LAND REFORM: A governmental policy that redistributes agricultural or residential land to those who live or work on that land.

LAUREATE: The recipient of an award for outstanding achievement. This word is derived from the ancient Greek and Roman practice of laying a laurel wreath around the neck of an honoree. Upon his death, Alfred Nobel, a Swedish businessman who made his fortune selling explosives, established the Nobel prizes in 1901 "to those who, during the preceding year, have conferred the greatest benefit to humankind." They include prizes in literature, physics, chemistry, medicine, economics, and peace.

LEAGUE OF NATIONS: Founded in 1920, the league was the first worldwide intergovernmental organization whose principal mission was to maintain world peace. The League of Nations formally dissolved in 1946, replaced by the United Nations.

MARTIAL LAW: The suspension of civil or constitutional law with imposition of military rule over normal government functions.

MARXISM: A political and economic theory developed by Karl Marx that views historical class struggle through an economic lens and envisions a future where everyone in society acts for the common good.

MERCENARY: A person who serves merely for wages and not any membership, loyalty, or belief; a soldier hired into service for personal profit.

MUFTI: A Sunni term for a high-raking cleric.

MULLAH: In Shia Islam, a lesser cleric.

NANSEN PASSPORT: An internationally recognized refugee travel document for stateless people, issued by the League of Nations between 1922 and 1938.

NATIONALISM: Strong identification with one nation to the point of placing its interests above those of anything else.

NATIONALIZATION: The seizure by a country of privately controlled companies that it then administers.

NEURODIVERSITY: The differences in brain function among individuals within society.

NIQAB: Muslim woman's veil that covers the mouth and nose. It is worn with a head scarf.

PASSING: In the American context, being regarded or accepted as a racial or ethnic group other than the one a person is born into.

PURDAH: From a Persian word meaning a religious and social practice of separating females. The practice occurs among some Muslim and Hindu communities. Women in purdah can be physically separated from men and also wear clothing that covers most of their bodies.

RAMAYANA: A classic text of ancient India containing myths and parables on how to lead an ethical life so that good always triumphs over evil.

RATIFY: To approve formally. When a country ratifies an international treaty, it agrees to be bound by it and adjusts its domestic laws to reflect the treaty obligations.

REALPOLITIK: Pragmatic or practical politics or diplomacy, as opposed to politics or diplomacy that prioritizes ideology or ethics.

REFUGEE: From the French, the term was first used to describe Protestants forced to flee France because of religious persecution in the late 1600s. The term now means anyone fleeing war, violence, or natural disaster.

REPATRIATE: To send someone back to their country of origin.

ROMA: Along with Rom and Romani, an Indo-Aryan people with a nomadic culture.

RUNNING OF THE BULLS: An annual festival in Spain and Portugal during which streets are fenced off and participants run with the bulls toward the bullring, where the bulls will later be ritually killed.

SELF-DETERMINATION: The process by which a people or nation determines its statehood, government, and laws.

SHARECROPPING: Legal arrangement by which a farmer works for a landowner in exchange for a fee or portion of the crop. In America, this system was considered an unfair extension of slavery and lasted well into the 20th century.

SMALL DONOR MODEL: To generate funding for a campaign or project by seeking small donations from individual persons versus soliciting corporate or government financing.

STUDENT NONVIOLENT COORDINATING COMMITTEE (SNCC): A civil rights group that emerged in 1960 from the student-led sit-ins at segregated lunch counters in Greensboro, North Carolina, and Nashville, Tennessee. SNCC coordinated and assisted direct-action challenges to segregation and the political exclusion of African Americans. The group had disbanded by 1973.

THIRD WORLD COUNTRIES: A term given to a large group of poor countries. The so-called first world consists of developed countries like the United States and France. So-called second world countries were allied with the Soviet Union.

UNITED NATIONS (UN): Formed in 1945 in the wake of World War II, the United Nations is an intergovernmental organization whose purpose is to foster peace and security, develop friendly relations among nations, and achieve international cooperation. It is the world's largest international organization. The main offices are in Geneva, Switzerland, and New York City. Dozens of other offices are throughout the world.

WAR PROFITEER: A company or person that makes enormous profits by selling weapons and supplies or by otherwise increasing business around armed conflicts.

SELECTED BIBLIOGRAPHY

Introduction

Adorno, Rolena. *Guamán Poma: Writing and Resistance in Colonial Peru.* Austin: University of Texas Press, 2000.

Anthony, Dani. "Bartolomé de las Casas and 500 Years of Racial Injustice." *Origins: Current Events in Historical Perspective* (July 2015).

Ellsberg, Robert. "Las Casas' Discovery: What the 'Protector of the Indians' Found in America." *America: The Jesuit Review of Faith & Culture* (November 5, 2012).

Hemming, John. *The Conquest of the Incas.* New York: Harcourt, Brace, Jovanovich, 1970.

Kirk, Robin, et al., eds. *The Peru Reader: History, Culture, Politics.* Durham: Duke University Press, 2005.

The Man in White: Henri Dunant

Dunant, Henry. *A Memory of Solferino.* Geneva, Switzerland: International Committee of the Red Cross, 1986.

Gumpert, Martin. *Dunant: The Story of the Red Cross.* Oxford, UK: Oxford University Press, 1938.

Moorehead, Caroline. *Dunant's Dream: War, Switzerland and the History of the Red Cross.* New York: Carroll & Graf Publishers, 1999.

NobelPrize.org. "The Nobel Peace Prize 1901," n.d. https://www.nobel prize.org/prizes/peace/1901/dunant/biographical/.

Europe's Conscience: Fridtjof Nansen

Facing History and Ourselves. "People Without Papers." Chap. 3 in *Holocaust and Human Behavior*. Memphis: Facing History and Ourselves, 2017. https://www.facinghistory.org/holocaust-and -human-behavior/chapter-3/people-without-papers.

Hieronymi, Otto. "The Nansen Passport: A Tool of Freedom of Movement and of Protection." *Refugee Survey Quarterly* 22, no. 1 (April 2003): 36–47.

Huntford, Roland. *Nansen: The Explorer as Hero*. New York: Barnes & Noble, 1988.

McCarthy. "Just a Life: The Story of Fridtjof Nansen," August 23, 2019. YouTube video, 1:26:04. https://www.youtube.com/watch?v =LAsMDA2sJbo.

Nansen, Fridtjof. *Farthest North: The Voyage of Exploration of the Fram and the Fifteen Month's Expedition*. London: Gibson Square, 2002.

——. *First Crossing of Greenland*. London: Gibson Square, 2001.

——. *In Northern Mists: Arctic Exploration in Early Times*. Vol. 1. London: William Heinemann, 1911. https://www.gutenberg.org /ebooks/40633.

——. "Nobel Lecture." NobelPrize.org, December 19, 1922. https://www .nobelprize.org/prizes/peace/1922/nansen/lecture/.

Nasaw, David. *The Last Million: Europe's Displaced Persons from World War to Cold War*. New York: Penguin Press, 2020.

Norwegian Refugee Council. "Fridtjof Nansen: A Man of Action and Vision," October 12, 2010. YouTube video, 4:33. https://www .youtube.com/watch?v=vR7_wNdxLac.

Sorensen, Jon. *The Saga of Fridtjof Nansen*. Translated by J. B. C. Watkins. New York: W. W. Norton, 1932.

Suny, Ronald Grigor. *"They Can Live in the Desert but Nowhere Else":* *A History of the Armenian Genocide.* Princeton, NJ: Princeton University Press, 2017.

Tooky History. "Fridtjof Nansen: The Arctic Saga," April 27, 2017. YouTube video, 3:13. https://www.youtube.com/watch?v=gUvzRWI8go0.

Utne, Eric, ed. *Brenda, My Darling: The Love Letters of Fridtjof Nansen to Brenda Ueland.* Minneapolis: Utne Institute, 2011.

The White Flame: Eglantyne Jebb

Becker, Jo. *Campaigning for Children: Strategies for Advancing Children's Rights.* Stanford, CA: Stanford University Press, 2017.

Freeman, Michael. *A Magna Carta for Children? Rethinking Children's Rights.* The Hamlyn Lectures. New York: Cambridge University Press, 2020.

Mahood, Linda. "Eglantyne Jebb: Remembering, Representing and Writing a Rebel Daughter." *Women's History Review* 17, no. 1 (February 1, 2008): 1–20.

———. *Feminism and Voluntary Action: Eglantyne Jebb and Save the Children, 1876–1928.* New York: Palgrave Macmillan, 2009.

Mulley, Clare. "The Forgotten Story of Eglantyne Jebb: The Woman Who Founded Save the Children." History Hit (website), March 22, 2019. https://www.historyhit.com/the-forgotten-story-of-eglantyne-jebb-the-woman-who-founded-save-the-children/.

———. *The Woman Who Saved the Children: A Biography of Eglantyne Jebb, Founder of Save the Children.* Oxford, UK: Oneworld Publications, 2009.

Wilson, Francesca M. *Rebel Daughter of a Country House: The Life of Eglantyne Jebb, Founder of the Save the Children Fund.* London: George Allen and Unwin, 1967.

The Towering Intellect: Peng Chun (P. C.) Chang

Glendon, Mary Ann. *A World Made New: Eleanor Roosevelt and the Universal Declaration of Human Rights,* New York: Random House, 2001.

Roth, Hans Ingvar. *P. C. Chang and the Universal Declaration of Human Rights.* Philadelphia: University of Pennsylvania Press, 2018.

Urquhart, Brian. "Mrs. Roosevelt's Revolution." Review of *A World Made New: Eleanor Roosevelt and the Declaration of Human Rights,* by Mary Ann Glendon. *New York Review of Books,* April 26, 2001.

Equality, Not Special Status: Hansa Mehta

Clinton, Hillary. "Hilary Clinton 'Women's Rights Are Human Rights' Speech at 1995 Women's Conference Beijing Transcript." Speech given at United Nations Fourth World Conference on Women, Beijing, China, September 5, 1995. Rev.com. Transcript and audio, 20:15. https://www.rev.com/blog/transcripts/hillary-clinton -womens-rights-are-human-rights-speech-at-1995-womens -conference-beijing-transcript.

Guha, Ramachandra. *India After Gandhi: The History of the World's Largest Democracy.* New York: Ecco, 2007.

Mehta, Hansa. *Indian Woman.* Delhi, India: Butala, 1981.

——. "Interview: Mrs Hansa Mehta (Part 1)." By Uma Shanker. Centre of South Asian Studies, September 10, 1969. https://www.s-asian.cam .ac.uk/archive/audio/item/interview-mrs-hansa-mehta-part-1/.

Nair, Smitha. "Video Series: How Hansa Mehta Influenced the Words in the UN Declaration of Human Rights." Scroll.in (website), January 26, 2018. Video, 2:57. https://scroll.in/video/866436/video-series -how-hansa-mehta-influenced-the-words-in-the-un-declaration -of-human-rights.

Newsd (website). "Hansa Jeevraj Mehta: Freedom Fighter, Reformer, Educator Who Fought for Gender Equality." April 4, 2019. https:// newsd.in/hansa-jeevraj-mehta-freedom-fighter-reformer-educator -who-fought-for-gender-equality/.

Radhakrishna, N. S. "Hansa Mehta Made Human Rights Truly Universal," February 11, 2021. https://www.easterneye.biz/hansa -mehta-made-human-rights-truly-universal/.

Masters of Their Fate: Carlos Peña Rómulo

Burke, Roland. "'The Compelling Dialogue of Freedom': Human Rights at the Bandung Conference." *Human Rights Quarterly* 28, no. 4 (November 2006): 947–65.

Pace, Eric. "Carlos Romulo of Philippines, a founder of U.N., Dies at 86." *New York Times*, December 15, 1985. https://www.nytimes .com/1985/12/15/us/carlos-romulo-of-philippines-a-founder-of -un-dies-at-86.html.

Rómulo, Beth Day, and David F. Hyatt. *The Writer, the Lover, and the Diplomat*. Mandaluyong City, Philippines: Anvil Publishing, 2015.

Rómulo, Carlos. *I Saw the Fall of the Philippines*. Garden City, NY: Doubleday, Doran & Company, 1942.

———. *I Walked with Heroes*. New York: Holt, Rinehart and Winston, 1961.

———. *The Meaning of Bandung*. Chapel Hill: University of North Carolina Press, 1956.

———. "One World or None." Speech given as part of "1950: Midpoint of the Century" lecture series, April 2, 1950. Published by NYPR Archive Collections. Podcast, 42:11. https://www.wnyc.org/story/the-philippine-nation/.

———. *The United*. New York: Crown Publishers, 1951.

Seville, Hope Christian. "Carlos P. Romulo: A Warrior for Peace." June 18, 2012. YouTube video, 15:38. https://www.youtube.com/watch?v=3L6u11uKDjw.

The Incurable Optimist: Ralph J. Bunche

Bunche, Ralph J., and Robert R. Edgar. *An African American in South Africa: The Travel Notes of Ralph J. Bunche*. Columbus: Ohio University Press, 2001.

Greaves, William, dir. *Ralph Bunche: An American Odyssey*. New York: Schomberg Center for Research in Black Culture, 2001.

Henry, Charles P. *Ralph Bunche: Model Negro or American Other?* New York: New York University Press, 1999.

Holloway, Jonathan Scott. *Confronting the Veil: Abram Harris Jr., E. Franklin Frazier, and Ralph Bunche, 1919–1941*. Chapel Hill: University of North Carolina Press, 2002.

Keppel, Ben. *The Work of Democracy: Ralph Bunche, Kenneth B. Clark, Lorraine Hansberry, and the Cultural Politics of Race*. Cambridge, MA: Harvard University Press, 1995.

UCLA Newsroom. "Ralph Bunche's Legacy: In His Own Words," August 6, 2019. Article and video, 3:46. http://newsroom.ucla.edu/stories/ralph-bunche-in-his-own-words.

Urquhart, Brian. *Ralph Bunche: An American Odyssey*. New York: W. W. Norton, 1998.

A Case for Humanity: Benjamin B. Ferencz

Avrich, Barry, dir. *Prosecuting Evil*. Toronto, ON: Melbar Entertainment Group, 2019.

Belzberg, Edet, dir. *Watchers of the Sky*. Brooklyn, NY: Propeller Films, 2015.

Ferencz, Benjamin. "Ferencz Interviewed by Russel Harvey." By Russel Harvey. *Almost Live*, episode 40, August 2, 1989. United States Holocaust Memorial Museum. Video, 30:33. https://collections.ushmm.org/search/catalog/irn1000978.

———. "Oral History Interview with Benjamin B. Ferencz." By Joan Ringelheim. United States Holocaust Memorial Museum, August 26 and October 21, 1994. Video, 16 parts, 5:04:35. https://collections.ushmm.org/search/catalog/irn507286.

———. "A Prosecutor's Personal Account—Nuremberg to Rome." September 23, 1998. Published in April 1999 by BenFerencz.org, https://benferencz.org/articles/1990-1999/a-prosecutors-personal-account-nuremberg-to-rome/.

Ferencz, Benjamin, and Antonio Cassese. *The Prosecutor and the Judge: Benjamin Ferencz and Antonio Cassese, Interviews and Writings*. Amsterdam: Pallas Publications, 2010.

Ferencz, Benjamin, and Ken Keyes. *Planethood: The Key to Your Future*. Coos Bay, OR: Vision Books, 1988.

Ferencz, Benjamin, and Telford Taylor. *Less Than Slaves: Jewish Forced Labor and the Quest for Compensation*. Bloomington: Indiana University Press, 2002.

Heller, Karen. "The Improbable Story of the Man Who Won History's 'Biggest Murder Trial' at Nuremberg." *Washington Post*, August 31, 2016.

Hofmann, Tom. *Benjamin Ferencz, Nuremberg Prosecutor and Peace Advocate*. Jefferson, NC: McFarland & Company, 2014.

United States Holocaust Memorial Museum. "US Forces Liberate Buchenwald." Article and video, 1:24. https://www.ushmm.org /learn/timeline-of-events/1942-1945/us-forces-liberate-buchenwald.

Imp, Crusader, Dude: Pauli Murray

Duke University. "Imp, Crusader, Dude, Priest: An Exhibit about the Life and Legacy of 20th Century Human Rights Champion Pauli Murray." n.d. https://sites.fhi.duke.edu/paulimurrayproject/.

Mack, Kenneth W. "Pauli Murray, Eleanor Roosevelt's Beloved Radical." Review of *The Firebrand and the First Lady: Portrait of a Friendship: Pauli Murray, Eleanor Roosevelt, and the Struggle for Social Justice*, by Patricia Bell-Scott. *Boston Review*, February 24, 2016. https:// bostonreview.net/books-ideas/kenneth-mack-patricia-bell-scott -firebrand-first-lady-pauli-murray-eleanor-roosevelt.

Murray, Pauli. *Pauli Murray: The Autobiography of a Black Activist, Feminist, Lawyer, Priest, and Poet*. Knoxville: The University of Tennessee Press, 1989.

———. *Proud Shoes: The Story of an American Family*. Boston: Beacon Press, 1999.

———. "States' Laws on Race and Color and Appendices: Containing International Documents, Federal Laws and Regulations, Local Ordinances and Charts." Cincinnati: Woman's Division of Christian

Service, Board of Missions and Church Extension, Methodist Church, 1950.

Murray, Pauli, and Elizabeth Alexander. *Dark Testament and Other Poems*. New York: Liveright, 2018.

Murray, Pauli, and Patricia Bell-Scott. *Song in a Weary Throat: Memoir of an American Pilgrimage*. New York: Liveright, 2018.

Rosenberg, Rosalind. *Jane Crow: The Life of Pauli Murray*. Oxford, UK: Oxford University Press, 2017.

Schulz, Kathryn. "The Many Lives of Pauli Murray." *New Yorker*, April 10, 2017. https://www.newyorker.com/magazine/2017/04/17/the-many -lives-of-pauli-murray.

Strum, Philippa. "Pauli Murray's Indelible Mark on the Fight for Equal Rights." American Civil Liberties Union, June 24, 2020. https:// www.aclu.org/issues/womens-rights/pauli-murrays-indelible-mark -fight-equal-rights.

Art as Protest: Víctor Jara

Espada, Martín. *His Hands Were Gentle: Selected Lyrics of Víctor Jara*. Middlesbrough, UK: Smokestack, 2012.

Fundación Victor Jara. 2017. https://fundacionvictorjara.org/.

Garrison, Cassandra. "Extradite Accused Killer of Chilean Singer Victor Jara, Daughter Pleads." Reuters, July 20, 2018. https://www.reuters .com/article/us-chile-rights-jara-idUSKBN1KA2MG.

Haberman, Clyde. "He Died Giving a Voice to Chile's Poor. A Quest for Justice Took Decades." *New York Times*, November 18, 2018. https:// www.nytimes.com/2018/11/18/us/victor-jara.html.

Jara, Joan. *An Unfinished Song: The Life of Victor Jara*. New York: Ticknor & Fields, 1984.

Jara, Víctor. "Concierto Víctor Jara en Perú—17 de Julio de 1973 (Recital Completo)." Filipe Rebolledo Sáez,July 9, 2014. YouTube video, 1:02:40. https://www.youtube.com/watch?v=UhXBrp3oAIM.

Jara, Víctor. "Victor Jara—'Móvil' Oil Special." Victor Jara—Música, December 22, 2014. YouTube video, 2:47. https://www.youtube.com /watch?v=aKagnr6UBQE.

Lynskey, Dorian. "Víctor Jara: The Folk Singer Murdered for His Music." BBC News, August 12, 2020. https://www.bbc.com/culture/article /20200812-vctor-jara-the-folk-singer-murdered-for-his-music.

Perlmutt, Bent-Jorgen, dir. *ReMastered: Massacre at the Stadium.* 2019; Los Angeles: All Rise Films.

Watts, Jonathan, and Jonathan Franklin. "Agony of Chile's Dark Days Continues as Murdered Poet's Wife Fights for Justice." *The Guardian,* September 11, 2013. http://www.theguardian.com/world/2013 /sep/11/chile-coup-anniversary-victor-jara-murder.

Determination, Patience, Insistence: Juan E. Méndez

Frohne, Lauren. "Torture: It Can Happen Anywhere." Open Society Foundations, February 13, 2014. Article and video, 2:15. https://www .opensocietyfoundations.org/voices/torture-it-can-happen-anywhere.

Méndez, Juan E. Center for Human Rights & Humanitarian Law. "Human Rights Defender: A Conversation with Professor Juan Mendez." Interview by Hadar Harris. August 7, 2014. YouTube video, 1:05:24. https://www.youtube.com/watch?v=BQNsKcfA8_4.

——. "Juan E. Méndez: 'We Have Lost a Sense of Purpose About Eliminating Torture.'" By Vivian Calderoni and Oliver Hudson. *Sur— International Journal on Human Rights* (July 2017): https://sur.conectas .org/en/juan-e-mendez-lost-sense-purpose-eliminating-torture/.

——. "'People Tell You What You Need to Know, Without Brutality': Former UN Torture Expert." By Natalie Hutchison. United Nations News, n.d. Audio, 13:44. https://soundcloud.com/unradio/people -tell-you-what-you-need-to-know-without-brutality-former-un -torture-expert.

——. "A Torture Victim Turned Human Rights Champion Ends His United Nations Run Fighting for Justice." By Jamil Dakwar. American Civil Liberties Union, November 4, 2016. https://www.aclu.org/blog /national-security/torture/torture-victim-turned-human-rights -champion-ends-his-un-run-fighting.

——. "U.N. Investigator Talks About the Future of Solitary and the Death Penalty." By Jamil Dakwar. American Civil Liberties Union, November 7, 2016. https://www.aclu.org/blog/human -rights/human-rights-and-death-penalty/un-investigator-talks -about-future-solitary-and.

Méndez, Juan E., and Marjory Wentworth. *Taking a Stand: The Evolution of Human Rights*. New York: St. Martin's Press, 2011.

Miami Law Staff. "Juan E. Méndez Speaks on the Connection of Human Rights During Henkin Lecture." University of Miami School of Law, February 17, 2021. https://www.law.miami.edu/news/2021/february /juan-e-m%C3%A9ndez-speaks-connection-human-rights-during -henkin-lecture.

The Tightrope Walker: Shirin Ebadi

Ebadi, Shirin. *The Golden Cage: Three Brothers, Three Choices, One Destiny*. San Diego: Kales Press, 2011.

——. *Refugee Rights in Iran*. London: Saqi Books, 2008.

———. "Shirin Ebadi, Nobel Peace Prize 2003: My Truth and Other Versions." Nobel Prize, September 11, 2020. YouTube video, 17:05. https://www.youtube.com/watch?v=opruzskQP6E.

———. "Shirin Ebadi: Who Defines Islam?" By Deniz Kandiyoti. openDemocracy, March 21, 2011. https://www.opendemocracy.net /en/5050/shirin-ebadi-who-defines-islam/.

———. *Until We Are Free: My Fight for Human Rights in Iran.* New York: Random House, 2016.

Ebadi, Shirin, and Azadeh Moaveni. *Iran Awakening: One Woman's Journey to Reclaim Her Life and Country.* New York: Random House, 2007.

Lichter, Ida. *Muslim Women Reformers: Inspiring Voices against Oppression.* Amherst, NY: Prometheus Books, 2009.

Nouraie-Simone, Fereshteh. *On Shifting Ground: Muslim Women in the Global Era.* New York: Feminist Press at the City University of New York, 2014.

Refusing to Be Silent: Judith Heumann

Aggeler, Madeleine. "How I Get It Done: Disability-Rights Activist Judy Heumann." The Cut, *New York*, September 28, 2020. https://www .thecut.com/2020/09/how-i-get-it-done-disability-rights-activist -judy-heumann.html.

Heumann, Judith. "Judith Heumann—Defying Obstacles in 'Being Heumann' and 'Crip Camp.'" By Trevor Noah. *The Daily Show.* March 10, 2020. YouTube video, 10:03. https://www.youtube.com /watch?v=ybcQbpSVo3c.

———. "Our Fight for Disability Rights—and Why We're Not Done Yet." Filmed at TEDxMidAtlantic, October 2016. TED video, 17:01. https:// www.ted.com/talks/judith_heumann_our_fight_for_disability _rights_and_why_we_re_not_done_yet.

Heumann, Judith, and Kristen Joiner. *Being Heumann: An Unrepentant Memoir of a Disability Rights Activist.* Boston: Beacon Press, 2020.

———. *Rolling Warrior: The Incredible, Sometimes Awkward, True Story of a Rebel Girl on Wheels Who Helped Spark a Revolution.* Boston: Beacon Press, 2021.

Lebrecht, James, and Nicole Newnham, dirs. *Crip Camp.* Chicago: Higher Ground Productions , 2020.

Schulze, Marianne, and Maya Sabatello, eds. *Human Rights and Disability Advocacy.* Philadelphia: University of Pennsylvania Press, 2014.

Shapiro, Joseph P. *No Pity: People with Disabilities Forging a New Civil Rights Movement.* New York: Times Books, 1994.

Humans Are Animals Are Humans: Ingrid Newkirk

Boyer, Peter J. "Horse Sense." *New Yorker*, April 27, 2009. https://www.newyorker.com/magazine/2009/05/04/horse-sense.

Carlson, Peter. "The Great Silver Spring Monkey Debate." *Washington Post*, February 24, 1991. https://www.washingtonpost.com/archive/lifestyle/magazine/1991/02/24/the-great-silver-spring-monkey-debate/25d3cc06-49ab-4a3c-afd9-d9eb35a862c3/.

Galkin, Matthew, dir. *I Am an Animal: The Story of Ingrid Newkirk and PETA.* New York: Stick Figure Productions, 2007.

Lawler, Andrew. "After Claims of Animal Cruelty, Can the Circus Survive?" *Smithsonian Magazine,* January 29, 2018. https://www.smithsonianmag.com/arts-culture/after-claims-of-animal-cruelty-can-circus-survive-180967954/.

Michelson, Brittany, and Ingrid Newkirk. *Voices for Animal Liberation: Inspirational Accounts by Animal Rights Activists.* New York: Skyhorse Publishing, 2020.

Newkirk, Ingrid. "Ingrid Newkirk: Animalkind," By Bill Maher. *Real Time with Bill Maher*, January 24, 2020. YouTube video, 8:54. https://www.youtube.com/watch?v=QTq-GlWxP5c.

——. "A Pragmatic Fight for Animal Rights." *The Guardian*, January 21, 2010. http://www.theguardian.com/commentisfree/cif-green/2010/jan/21/peta-animal-rights-campaign.

——. *Free the Animals: The Story of the Animal Liberation Front*. Lantern Books, 2000.

Newkirk, Ingrid, and Gene Stone. *Animalkind: Remarkable Discoveries About Animals and Revolutionary New Ways to Show Them Compassion*. New York: Simon & Schuster, 2020.

Younge, Gary. "We're Stunt Queens. We Have to Be." *The Guardian*, February 23, 2006. http://www.theguardian.com/uk/2006/feb/24/animalwelfare.comment.

Reclaiming the Meaning of Peace: Jody Williams

American Friends Service Committee. "Nobel Peace Laureates Publish the Hiroshima Declaration on the Abolition of Nuclear Weapons," November 15, 2010. https://www.afsc.org/document/nobel-peace-laureates-publish-hiroshima-declaration-abolition-nuclear-weapons.

Channareth, Tun. "Getting to Know Tun Channareth." Interview by *Arms Control Today*. Arms Control Association, April 3, 2014. https://www.armscontrol.org/act/2014-07/getting-know-tun-channareth.

Faulkner, Frank. *Moral Entrepreneurs and the Campaign to Ban Landmines*. New York: Rodopi, 2007.

Williams, Jody. *My Name Is Jody Williams: A Vermont Girl's Winding Path to the Nobel Peace Prize.* Berkeley: University of California Press, 2013.

——. "Q&A: Nobel Peace Prize Winner Jody Williams on What It Takes to Change the World." By Emily Sernaker. *Ms. Magazine,* September 11, 2017. https://msmagazine.com/2017/09/11/qa-nobel -peace-prize-winner-jody-williams/.

——. "Q&A with Jody Williams." By Brian Lamb. C-SPAN, February 13, 2013. Transcript and video, 59:00. https://www.c-span.org/video /?310955-1/qa-jody-williams.

——. "A Realistic Vision for World Peace." Filmed at TEDWomen, December 2010. TED video, 10:36. https://www.ted.com/speakers /jody_williams.

The Long Road: S. James Anaya
Anaya, S. James. "Copper Mine Will Hurt Tribes and the Environment." *Arizona Republic,* December 28, 2014. https://www.azcentral.com /story/opinion/op-ed/2014/12/29/resolution-copper-con/20865771/.

——. *Indigenous Peoples in International Law.* New York: Oxford University Press, 2004.

——. *International Human Rights and Indigenous Peoples.* New York: Aspen Publishers, 2009.

——. "James Anaya, UN Special Rapporteur on the Rights of Indigenous Peoples, Visits NCAI." National Congress of American Indians. YouTube video, 3:41. https://www.youtube.com/watch?v=DbBCYqSDr0M.

——. "Nicaragua's Titling of Communal Lands Marks Major Step for Indigenous Rights." UNSR. Jamessanaya.org, January 5, 2009. https:// unsr.jamessanaya.org/?p=113.

Bens, Jonas. *The Indigenous Paradox: Rights, Sovereignty, and Culture in the Americas*. Philadelphia: University of Pennsylvania Press, 2020.

Flavelle, Christopher, and Kalen Goodluck. "Dispossessed, Again: Climate Change Hits Native Americans Especially Hard." *New York Times*, June 27, 2021, https://www.nytimes.com/2021/06/27/climate /climate-Native-Americans.html.

Hurwitz, Deena, and Douglas Ford. *Human Rights Advocacy Stories*. St. Paul: Foundation Press, 2008.

RPM Admin. "The Last Speech of Deskaheh." *Real People's Media* (blog), November 1, 2016. https://realpeoples.media/the-last-speech -of-deskaheh/.

Young, Stephen. "Re-Historicising Dissolved Identities: Deskaheh, the League of Nations, and International Legal Discourse on Indigenous Peoples." *London Review of International Law* 7, no. 3 (November 2019): 377–408. https://doi.org/10.1093/lril/lraa004.

The Reporter: Anna Politkovskaya

Chalupa, Irena. "A Friend's Film Tribute to Anna Politkovskaya Premieres in Moscow." Radio Free Europe, December 2, 2011. https://www .rferl.org/a/friends_film_tribute_to_politokskaya_premieres_in _moscow/24409978.html.

Filatova, Irina. "Who Killed Anna Politkovskaya?" *The Guardian*, February 21, 2009. http://www.theguardian.com/commentisfree/2009/feb/20 /anna-politkovskaya-russia.

Klakström, Josie. "The Assassination of Anna Politkovskaya." Medium (website), July 30, 2020. https://medium.com/the-true-crime-edition /the-assassination-of-anna-politkovskaya-21b4c70bbe8d.

PEN America. "Anna Politkovskaya," October 6, 2015. https://pen.org /advocacy-case/anna-politkovskaya/.

Politkovskaya, Anna. *A Dirty War : A Russian Reporter in Chechnya.* Translated and edited by John Crowfoot. London: Harvill, 2001.

———. *Is Journalism Worth Dying For?: Final Dispatches.* Translated by Arch Tait. Brooklyn: Melville House, 2011.

———. *Nothing But the Truth: Selected Dispatches.* London: Harvill Secker, 2010.

———. *Putin's Russia.* London: Harvill Press, 2004.

———. *A Small Corner of Hell: Dispatches from Chechnya.* Translated by Alexander Burry and Tatiana Tulchinsky. Chicago: University of Chicago Press, 2007.

Politkovskaya, Anna, and Scott Simon. *A Russian Diary: A Journalist's Final Account of Life, Corruption, and Death in Putin's Russia.* Translated by Arch Tait. New York: Random House, 2007.

The Accidental Environmentalist: Catherine Coleman Flowers

Center for Earth Ethics. "Catherine Flowers," n.d. https://centerforearth ethics.org/catherine-flowers/.

Connor, Shelley. "UN Rapporteur Reports Extreme Poverty 'Unseen in the First World' in Alabama." World Socialist Web Site, December 13, 2017. https://www.wsws.org/en/articles/2017/12/13/sewa-d13.html.

Flowers, Catherine Coleman. "Hands Across the Water: Catherine Flowers' Quest to Drain the Septic Swamp." By Judith Lewis Mernit. *Salon*, January 5, 2021. https://www.salon.com/2021/01/05/hands-across-the -water-catherine-flowers-quest-to-drain-the-septic-swamp_partner/.

———. "Q&A: An Environmental Justice Champion's Journey from Rural Alabama to Biden's Climate Task Force." By Ilana Cohen. *Inside Climate*

News, July 10, 2020. https://insideclimatenews.org/news/10072020
/catherine-coleman-flowers-environmental-justice-q-and-a/.

———. *Waste.* New York: The New Press, 2020.

Okeowo, Alexis. "The Heavy Toll of the Black Belt's Wastewater
Crisis." *New Yorker,* November 23, 2020. https://www.newyorker
.com/magazine/2020/11/30/the-heavy-toll-of-the-black-belts-waste
water-crisis.

Sacred Rivers: Berta Cáceres

Democracy Now! "Remembering Berta Cáceres, Assassinated Honduras
Indigenous & Environmental Leader." March 4, 2016. YouTube
video, 14:51. https://www.youtube.com/watch?v=dQWywN6553Y.

———. "Part 2: Berta Cáceres' Daughter: US Military Aid Has Fueled
Repression & Violence in Honduras." March 18, 2016. YouTube
video, 26:19. https://www.youtube.com/watch?v=14Toi22S5fY.

Friends of the Earth International. "Cancel the Agua Zarca Project in
Honduras." Video, 2:04. https://www.foei.org/agua-zarca.

Goldman Environmental Foundation. "Berta Cáceres," n.d. https://www
.goldmanprize.org/recipient/berta-caceres/.

Grandin, Greg. "Before Her Murder, Berta Cáceres Singled Out Hillary
Clinton for Criticism." *The Nation,* March 10, 2016. https://www.the
nation.com/article/chronicle-of-a-honduran-assassination-foretold/.

Lakhani, Nina. "Berta Cáceres: Seven Men Convicted of Murdering
Honduran Environmentalist." *The Guardian,* November 29, 2018.
https://www.theguardian.com/world/2018/nov/29/berta-caceres
-seven-men-convicted-conspiracy-murder-honduras.

———. "Honduras Dam Project Shadowed by Violence." Al Jazeera, December 24, 2013. https://www.aljazeera.com/features/2013/12/24 /honduras-dam-project-shadowed-by-violence.

———. *Who Killed Berta Cáceres? Dams, Death Squads, and an Indigenous Defender's Battle for the Planet.* London: Verso, 2020.

Mackey, Danielle. "Drugs, Dams, and Power: The Murder of Honduran Activist Berta Cáceres." The Intercept, March 11, 2016. https://the intercept.com/2016/03/11/drugs-dams-and-power-the-murder-of -honduran-activist-berta-caceres/.

UN News. "Honduras Risks Becoming 'Lawless Killing Zone' for Human Rights Defenders—UN Expert." March 18, 2016. https://news .un.org/en/story/2016/03/524762-honduras-risks-becoming -lawless-killing-zone-human-rights-defenders-un-expert.

Zinn Education Project. "Berta Cáceres: Environmental Organizer," n.d. https://www.zinnedproject.org/materials/berta-caceres-environmental -organizer/.

The Tigress: FannyAnn Eddy

Cherry, Kittredge. "FannyAnn Eddy: Lesbian Martyr in Africa." *Q Spirit* (blog), last updated September 29, 2021. https://qspirit.net /fannyann-eddy-lesbian-martyr-africa/.

Darling, Laura. "FannyAnn Viola Eddy: Speaking Against Silence." Making Queer History, n.d. https://www.makingqueerhistory.com /articles/2016/12/20/fannyann-viola-eddy-speaking-against-silence.

Eddy, FannyAnn. "Testimony by FannyAnn Eddy at the UN Commission on Human Rights," October 4, 2004. https://www.hrw .org/news/2004/10/04/testimony-fannyann-eddy-un-commission -human-rights.

Ericsson, Filip. "Remembering Fanny Ann Eddy." *World Politics Uncovered* (blog), November 23, 2015. https://worldpoliticsuncovered.wordpress.com/2015/11/23/remembering-fannyann-eddy/.

Hoffman, Danny. *The War Machines: Young Men and Violence in Sierra Leone and Liberia.* Durham, NC: Duke University Press, 2011.

Human Rights Watch. "African Voices Celebrate LGBT Equality." May 16, 2014. https://www.hrw.org/news/2014/05/16/african-voices-celebrate-lgbt-equality.

———. "Sierra Leone: Lesbian Rights Activist Brutally Murdered," October 5, 2004. https://www.hrw.org/news/2004/10/05/sierra-leone-lesbian-rights-activist-brutally-murdered.

Jacob, Raouf J., dir. *A Culture of Silence.* Waltham, MA: Worldwide Cinema Frames, 2014.

King, Hobart M. "Blood Diamonds—Conflict Diamonds: What Is the Kimberley Process?" Geology.com, n.d. https://geology.com/articles/blood-diamonds.shtml.

Morgan, Ruth, and Saskia Wieringa, eds. *Tommy Boys, Lesbian Men, and Ancestral Wives: Female Same-Sex Practices in Africa.* Johannesburg, South Africa: Jacana Media, 2005. https://find.library.duke.edu/catalog/DUKE008604761.

Sierra Leone Truth and Reconciliation Commission. "Sierra Leone TRC Reports: Table of Contents," n.d. http://sierraleonetrc.org/index.php/view-the-final-report/download-table-of-contents.

Traub, James. "The Worst Place on Earth," *New York Review*, June 29, 2000. http://www.nybooks.com/articles/2000/06/29/the-worst-place-on-earth/.